MW00948941

PRAY-THROUGH PRAYERS TO DEFEAT ATTACKS AGAINST DESTINY

PRAY-THROUGH PRAYERS TO DEFEAT ATTACKS AGAINST DESTINY

SIDNEY EDI-OSAGIE

authorHOUSE®

AuthorHouse™
1663 Liberty Drive
Bloomington, IN 47403
www.authorhouse.com
Phone: 1 (800) 839-8640

© 2015 Sidney Edi-Osagie. All rights reserved.

No part of this book may be reproduced, stored in a retrieval system, or transmitted by any means without the written permission of the author.

Published by AuthorHouse 08/07/2015

ISBN: 978-1-5049-2797-0 (sc)
ISBN: 978-1-5049-2798-7 (hc)
ISBN: 978-1-5049-2799-4 (e)

Library of Congress Control Number: 2015912748

Print information available on the last page.

Any people depicted in stock imagery provided by Thinkstock are models, and such images are being used for illustrative purposes only. Certain stock imagery © Thinkstock.

This book is printed on acid-free paper.

Scripture quotations marked NKJV are taken from the New King James Version. Copyright © 1982 by Thomas Nelson, Inc. Used by permission. All rights reserved.

Scripture quotations marked NIV are taken from the Holy Bible, New International Version®. NIV®. Copyright © 1973, 1978, 1984 by International Bible Society. Used by permission of Zondervan. All rights reserved. [Biblica]

Scripture quotations marked NLT are taken from the Holy Bible, New Living Translation, copyright © 1996, 2004, 2007. Used by permission of Tyndale House Publishers, Inc. Carol Stream, Illinois 60188. All rights reserved. Website

Unless otherwise indicated, all scripture quotations are from The Holy Bible, English Standard Version® (ESV®). Copyright ©2001 by Crossway Bibles, a division of Good News Publishers. Used by permission. All rights reserved.

Contents

Part II.   Miracle Healing Confessions & Prayers

Part III. Destiny-Molding Prayers & Exhortations

Part IV. Life-Changing Prayers & Supplications

Welcome Note

Thank you for choosing to pray these prayers and meditate on the exhortations contained in *'Pray-Through Prayers To Defeat Attacks Against Destiny'*. The prayers and exhortations contained in this book are the result of years of devoted research and communing with the Holy Spirit. If you want to develop your prayer life and ensure victory in all areas of life and endeavor, this is the book to carefully study and pray. This anointed book is not only detailed and professionally compiled, but also designed to help you see results when you apply the principles shared.

Pastor Sidney Edi-Osagie

Dedication

I dedicate this book to my Best Friend and Strength, the Mighty Holy Spirit, and to all the Pastors, Evangelists, Ministers and Workers who labor tirelessly in God's vineyard.

Acknowledgements

To my wonderful family - Lami, David, Samuelle and Emmanuel. Thanks for your love and support!

To Christian "Chrissy" Dernbach, Irene Asante-Boadi Snr., Erhi Oputu and every other person who contributed in one way or the other in making this project a success.

To the entire City On The Hill Church Family, I appreciate your continued encouragement and support!

Preface

Pray-Through Prayers To Defeat Attacks Against Your Destiny is an anointed detailed prayer resource guide for those interested in winning the battle of the spirit and taking their prayer life to the next level. The truth is nothing happens in the realm of the physical without spiritual establishment; so if we fail to understand and carefully execute the battle in the spirit, we cannot adequately address the problems we face in the physical, and there may be no trophies to show for our time here on earth.

Our prayer lives are an indication of our relationship with God, and are closely tied to our relationships with our Bibles. You can't think or speak like someone you do not know or haven't spent considerable time practicing the way they speak, or else your language and expressions would be off; even if you intended to learn from that person.

God being our Father teaches and mentors us in the art of prayer through His loving Holy Spirit. The Spirit empowers us to pray according to God's will and also reveals strategies on how to get through to God in prayer, and the ways in which He responds to our prayers. Prayer is so important that Jesus' entire earthly ministry was empowered and sustained by it. He learned to pray from when He was a young lad, and became more effective in His prayer life when the Holy Spirit descended upon Him like a dove after His water baptism. Christ prayed all night for direction in selecting His disciples; He prayed for hours before walking on water towards His disciples; and prayed fervently in Gethsemane for strength and encouragement to be able to fulfill His divine assignment; and also cried out in supplication on the Cross, quoting the Scripture, "Father, Father, why have You forsaken Me?"

If God's Son or God Himself in the person of His Son operated solely on the basis of prayer, no believer has any other choice, if they wish to be effective in their earthly pilgrimage.

Introduction

The principle of prayer draws from the practice of communicating with God on the basis of His Word. Therefore, except it is grounded in Scripture, there is no other foundation for the prayer communion to be fully potent and effective. As such, each subtitle in this book, after the initial definitions are tied to Scriptural references to further enlighten the reader on the Biblical basis for the prayers in question. The Bible is a book of prayer, and the grandest one out there, given to man to fulfill his divine mandate. Where else can our content and revelation come from, except this Everlasting Book of Life?

Pray-Through Prayers to Defeat Attacks Against Destiny is a combination of detailed and powerful prayers for most of life's situations and attacks. The compilation of these prayers is based on the inspiration and leading of the Spirit of God and these prayers have been proven and tested with positive results and life changing testimonies. The Holy Spirit knows the immediate and future needs and challenges of man, so He is best suited to instruct and guide us in our approach to prayer (Romans 8:26-28).

In Memory Of

In loving memory of my mother
CHIEF CATHERINE NDIDI EDI-OSAGIE
(15 JAN 1934 – 16 FEB 2008)
who laid the foundation for my Christian walk
and willingness to answer
the call of God

The Wonders & Advantages of Prayer

1. God wants to hear from you
   - Isaiah 1:18-19
   - Numbers 10:9
   - Psalm 50:15

2. Prayer is simply a two-way communication between man and God
   - Jeremiah 33:3
   - Isaiah 65:24

3. Prayer produces power for supernatural transformation
   - 1 John 1:9
   - Psalm 51:10-12
   - Ephesians 4:29

4. Prayer connects the natural with the supernatural
   - Luke 9:28-31

5. The Word of God is the prescribed language for prayer
   - 1 John 5:14-15
   - Hebrews 9:16-17(NLT)
   - Matthew 4:1-11

6. Call God's cell phone through prayer before you call anyone else
   - Psalm 63:1-2
   - Psalm 91:15
   - Isaiah 55:6

7. In the place of prayer deep secrets are revealed
   - Deuteronomy 29:29
   - Proverbs 25:2
   - Daniel 2:22
   - Psalm 25:14
   - Jeremiah 33:3

8. Prayer is an indication of our complete dependence on God
   - Jeremiah 10:23
   - John 15:5
   - Philippians 2:13

9. Nothing is too little to pray about
   - Philippians 4:6
   - 1 Thessalonians 5:18
   - Jeremiah 32:27

10. Jesus prayed all night to choose the right set of disciples
    - Luke 6:12-13

11. We ought to worry less and pray more
    - Matthew 6:27-36
    - Philippians 4:6-7

12. We ought to pray and not give up
    - Luke 18:1-7

13. Persistence produces perseverance, and is proof of faith
    - Romans 5:3-4
    - 1 Peter 1:6-7
    - James 1:2-4

14. Prayer should not be seasonal, but all the time
    - 1 Thessalonians 5:17
    - Ephesians 6:18

15. Prayer builds intimacy between us and God
    - Psalm 63:1-11
    - James 4:8

16. Intimacy must be established and maintained
    - Deuteronomy 6:5
    - Jeremiah 31:3
    - John 17:22-23
    - Psalm 42:1-2

17. Prayer brings results, as it is one of heaven's most effective ways of producing change in the universe
    - Zephaniah 3:17
    - Ezekiel 22:30

18. Prayer and fasting can achieve extra-ordinary results
    - Matthew 6:17-18
    - Isaiah 58:5-7

19. Wrong Uses Of Prayer:

    A. Prayer is not to destroy enemies
    - Luke 9:51-56
    - Matthew 5:43-45

    B. Prayer is not for showing off
    - Matthew 6:5-6
    - Matthew 23:5

    C. Prayer should not be to impress others
    - 1 Thessalonians 2:4
    - John 4:24
    - Matthew 6:24
    - Luke 6:26

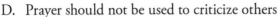

D. Prayer should not be used to criticize others
-   Matthew 7:1-5
-   Luke 18:10-14

E. Prayer is not for being vindictive
-   Mark 11:25
-   Luke 6:28

F. Prayer most times has some verbal expressions and physical manifestations, but prayer is also a spiritual and internal affair
-   1 Samuel 1:13
-   1 Samuel 16:1-6
-   Matthew 6:6

20. Factors that block answered prayer:

A. Sinful lifestyle
-   Proverbs 15:8
-   Isaiah 59:1-2

B. Unbelief
-   Mark 11:24
-   Hebrews 11:6

C. Doubt
-   Mark 11:23
-   James 1:5-8

D. Prayerlessness or not praying enough
-   Luke 18:1
-   James 4:2

21. Factors that facilitate answered prayer:

A. Repentance or Penitence
-   2 Chronicles 7:14

- Micah 7:19
- 1 John 1:5-9

B. Faith
- Hebrews 11:1-6
- Hebrews 4:1-3
- Hebrews 10:28

C. Being specific
- Matthew 7:7
- Matthew 21:22
- James 4:3

D. Perseverance
- 2 Thessalonians 3:13
- Luke 11:5-10
- Luke 18:1

E. Persistence
- Galatians 6:9
- Matthew 7:7-8 (AMP.)
- Proverbs 24:16

F. Aggression/Passion
- Matthew 11:12
- James 5:16
- Revelations 3:16

G. Following the blueprint God has laid for answered prayer
- Matthew 6:9-15
- Luke 11:9-13
- Romans 8:32
- Hebrews 4:16
- 2 Peter 1:3

Practice Made Perfect

The Constant Practice of Prayer Makes For
Perfection & Excellence In Prayer

1. The study of God's Word is necessary since prayer is essentially praying the will of God as expressed in God's Word
   - 2 Timothy 2:15
   - Colossians 3:16

2. Confession and verbal expression is inevitable in the art of prayer
   - Joshua 1:8
   - Proverbs 18:20-21

3. The continuous practice of prayer is a must if we are to master the art of prayer
   - James 2:14-26 (NLT)
   - Matthew 7:21-23

4. Talk is cheap; so when we have prayed we have to act in faith regarding the things we have prayed about
   - Matthew 21:28-32
   - Hebrews 11:6

5. Your practice of God's Words in the place of prayer makes for the fulfillment of your Christian destiny
   - John 13:12-17

6. What does the statement "Without faith it is impossible to please God really mean" (Hebrews 11:6)?
   - Faith is the key to successful fellowship with God and our fellow man, because faith is the key to taking God at His Word before, during and after we bring our petition to Him
   - 1 John 5:14-15
   - James 2:18

7. Faith and the Israelite testimony
   - Hebrews 4:1-2
   - Hebrews 11:1-39

8. Paul told the Philippians to keep their minds on good, godly, and positive things
   - Philippians 4:8-9 (NKJV; NLT)

9. Paul told Timothy to endure trials as a soldier and remember the scriptures he learned from his childhood
   - 2 Timothy 3:14-15
   - 2 Timothy 2:1-7

Warfare Prayers

These prayers are strictly geared at demolishing strongholds, and scattering the powers of darkness, wherever we find them. It is our prayer and hope that these should be done with profound passion, zeal and violence, for with such, results are guaranteed. Various themes are covered in this section, with emphasis on dominion and breakthrough prayers. (Matthew 11:12). The memory verses can also be confessed as prayers.

Raising The Standard Against The Enemy

<u>Scripture Reading</u>: Isaiah 59:19; Psalm 125:3; Proverbs 14:19; Jeremiah 20:11 (KJV)

<u>Memory Verse/Confession</u>: Isaiah 27:1

> *"In that day the Lord with His severe sword, great and strong, will punish Leviathan the fleeing serpent, Leviathan that twisted serpent; and He will slay the reptile that is in the sea."*

<u>Explanation:</u>

A standard has been raised against the evil one and his works, and that standard was raised at Calvary where Christ dealt a final blow of defeat against satan and his hold on humanity. Because this work was finished on the cross, we have a platform of victory from which we operate, and that platform is "Christ".

THEME: THE STANDARD HAS BEEN RAISED

1. I raise the standard of the Holy Ghost against every flood of affliction that has risen against me, in the name of Jesus (Isaiah 59:19).
2. Power of the Holy Spirit, overturn every verdict of wickedness pronounced against me, in the name of Jesus (Micah 3:8; Lamentations 3:37).
3. Anointing to soar above every wind of attack, come upon me now, in the name of Jesus
4. (Isaiah 40:31).

5. Finger of God, ruin and frustrate every advance of the gates of hell against my life, in the name of Jesus (Matthew 16:18; Exodus 8:16-19).

6. Prince of Peace, cut the wings of every prince of the power of the air flying against my destiny, in the name of Jesus (Ephesians 2:1-2).

7. Serpent of the Lord, swallow the serpent of every pharaoh attacking my life, in the name of Jesus (Exodus 7:10-12; Job 20:15)

8. Fisher angels of the Most High God, locate every marine habitation where my blessings are being held, and begin to retrieve everything the enemy has stolen from me, in the name of Jesus (Hebrew 1:14; Jeremiah 16:16)

9. Favor that wears out and outlives the attack of the enemy, locate and change my testimony, in the name of Jesus (Psalm 5:12; Psalm 103:12)

10. The Bible says the name of the Lord is a "Strong Tower", therefore I lift up the name of the Lord against every name and authority being invoked against my progress, in the name of Jesus (Proverbs 18:10; Philippians 2:10-11)

11. I strip the wicked of every weapon and any ammunition they are currently using against my wellbeing, in the name of Jesus (Job 5:12; Isaiah 44:25)

Releasing Confusion Into The Camp Of The Enemy

Scripture Reading: John 16:13; 2 Timothy 2:7; 1 Corinthians 14:33; Philippians 4:8-9

Memory Verse/Confession: 1 Samuel 14:20

> *"Then Saul and all the people who were with him assembled, and they went to the battle; and indeed every man's sword was against his neighbor, and there was very great confusion."*

Explanation:

Confusion is designed here to foster disagreement in the camp of the wicked. Because two can only work together when they agree, confusion renders the camp and works of the enemy ineffective. As such, we prescribe heavy doses of confusion in every camp of the enemy and we render them too confused to think straight, in Jesus' Name.

THEME: NO PEACE FOR THE WICKED

1. I release confusion into the camp of my enemies and I command them to be confounded, in the name of Jesus (Psalm 55:9)
2. Let every unrepentant adversary enter into divine error and destroy themselves, in the name of Jesus (2 Chronicles 20:22-24; Revelations 13:10)
3. I command everything that is currently making my enemies agree to confuse them and cause them to disagree, in the name of Jesus (Amos 3:3; Isaiah 19:1-3)

4. O Lord, introduce confusion in the rank and file of the army of the wicked, and cause them to begin to break ranks, in Jesus name (Deuteronomy 28:7, 20)

5. I fire the arrow of confusion into every satanic altar assigned to handle my case, in Jesus name (Exodus 23:27)

6. Holy Spirit, pollute every device of the wicked being used to monitor me with the spam of the blood of Jesus, in the name of Jesus (Revelations 12:11)

7. Father Lord, confuse my enemies that when I am behind they will be searching for me in front and when I'm in front they will searching for me behind, in Jesus name (Isaiah 41:11-KJV)

8. I confuse the vision, hearing and counsel of the wicked regarding my destiny and affairs, in the name of Jesus (2 Samuel 15:31)

9. O Lord, confuse and render null and void, every foundational witchcraft oracle speaking against my destiny, in the name of Jesus (Isaiah 45:16)

10. I bring complete confusion and disagreement amongst every ungodly gathering against me and command them to scatter, in the name of Jesus (Genesis 11:5-9; Isaiah 54:15)

Attacking Satanic Partnerships & Agreements

<u>Scripture Reading</u>: Isaiah 31:3; 1 Corinthians 15:33; Proverbs 13:20; Psalm 26:4-6

<u>Memory Verse/Confession</u>: Joshua 10:5

> *"Therefore the five kings of the Amorites, the king of Jerusalem, the king of Hebron, the king of Jarmuth, the king of Lachish, and the king of Eglon, gathered together and went up, they and all their armies, and camped before Gibeon and made war against it.*

<u>Explanation</u>:

God specializes in confusing and scattering the gatherings of the wicked. His Word rightly tells us that the wicked will surely gather, but assures us that they who gather against us will fall for our sake. Also, it is wise to choose your alliances and partnerships wisely, and the best way to achieve this is with the guidance of the Holy Spirit. Those who heed this counsel save themselves a lot of heartache.

THEME: IT SHALL NOT STAND

1. I attack and scatter every bond formed to attack my destiny, in the name of Jesus
2. (Jeremiah 7:5-7)
3. Every partnership that is not of God working against my glory, receive divine disgrace in Jesus name (Mark 6:7-NIV); Isaiah 49:9-NIV)

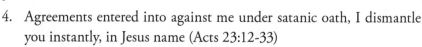

4. Agreements entered into against me under satanic oath, I dismantle you instantly, in Jesus name (Acts 23:12-33)

5. Every power using the elements to manipulate and attack me, I frustrate you by the blood of Jesus (Hebrews 2:14-15; Hebrews 12:24)

6. I overturn the effect of every ungodly alliance with the sun, moon and stars against me, in Jesus name (Colossians 1:13-14; Romans 8:37-39)

7. Let every partnership with powers of the waters against me, begin to backfire, in the name of Jesus (Job 5:12-14; Isaiah 44:24-25-KJV)

8. Holy Spirit, identify and neutralize every agreement fostered to destroy my career and relationships, in Jesus name (Isaiah 54:15)

9. I receive the power to arise and shine beyond every partnership formed against me, in Jesus name (Colossians 2:15; 1 John 2:13-14; John 10:19)

10. Wicked gathering constituted to harass and terrorize my destiny, be dismantled by the east wind of God, in Jesus name (Isaiah 54:14; Exodus 14:21)

11. Every evil unity of powers from all realms of darkness united against my greatness, collide with the Eternal Rock of Ages and be ground to powder, in the name of Jesus (Matthew 21:44; Isaiah 26:4-5-NLT)

12. Lord, I ask that you would give me discernment regarding all alliances and partnerships in my life, ministry and business, and also forgive me for not consulting you first before entering into such alliances, in Jesus name (Proverbs 3:5-6)

Release From Personal & Marital Bondage

<u>Scripture Reading</u>: Psalm 91:1-16; Isaiah 49:24-26; Psalm 20:1-8; Amos 3:3

<u>Memory verse/Confession</u>: Psalm 35:4-9

> *"Let those be turned back and brought to confusion who plot my hurt. Let them be like chaff before the wind and let the angel of the LORD chase them. Let their way be dark and slippery, and let the angel of the LORD pursue them. For without cause they have hidden their net for me in a pit, which they have dug without cause for my life. Let destruction come upon him unexpectedly, and let his net that he has hidden catch himself; into that very destruction let him fall. And my soul shall be joyful in the LORD; It shall rejoice in His salvation."*

<u>Explanation</u>:

Personal and marital issues are problems that can adversely affect anyone. The book Ecclesiastes clearly reveals the effects of this type of oppression when it states in Ecclesiastes 7:7A (KJV), "Surely oppression maketh a wise man mad." The New King James Version renders the same Scripture Verse as follows, "Surely oppression destroys a wise man's reason." The truth is any demonic influence or harassment that tends to manipulate or undermine you or your marriage is trying to destroy you personally so aggressive prayer is required.

THEME: POSSESSING MY MARITAL POSSESSION

1. Anyone who has known me intimately and has sworn to destroy me, destroy yourself, in Jesus name (Proverbs 11:8)
2. Every person who has benefitted from me and is attacking my destiny, receive the judgment of God, in Jesus name (Proverbs 17:13)
3. Holy Spirit, judge and condemn every altar from my father and mothers side and my husband's father and mothers side, speaking against my marital progress, in Jesus name (Judges 6:25-27)
4. Every ancestral serpentine covenant warring against my marriage and destiny, break and release me now, in Jesus name (Galatians 3:13)
5. Blood of Jesus and the liquid fire of the Holy Ghost, identify, melt and purge out every evil deposit in my system left by any spirit wife/husband, in the name of Jesus (Psalm 18:44-45; Revelations 12:11; Deuteronomy 4:24)
6. I cough up and vomit any poison and evil food eaten from the table of the enemy, in the name of Jesus (Matthew 15:13)
7. Any man or woman investing in my downfall, perish in my place, in the name of Jesus (Revelations 13:10)
8. Every person attacking my destiny and marriage who has lived with me or benefitted from me in the past, be exposed and disgraced, in Jesus name (Daniel 2:22; 2 Thessalonians 1:6)
9. Any power or personality that has sworn that over their dead body will my marriage work, receive the arrow of sudden death, in Jesus name (Psalm 35:1-9)
10. Evil altars raised against the success of my marriage, I pull you down by fire, in the land of the living, in Jesus name (Hebrews 12:29)
11. Fire of deliverance, begin to burn from the crown of my head/husband's head to the soul of my feet/husband's feet, in the name of Jesus (Obadiah 1:17)
12. Any strange woman/man troubling my marriage, receive disgrace by fire and leave my spouse alone, in Jesus name (Proverbs 2:11-20-KJV;
13. In the place where it has been said it shall not be well with me and my marriage, let it be said that this is (Your Name Here), who is blessed of The Lord, in Jesus name (Job 22:27-30-KJV)

14. Every invisible evil wall standing between me and my spouse understanding and agreeing with each other, be pulled down by fire, in Jesus name (Amos 3:3)

15. Any strong man or woman stubbornly sitting on my marital peace and settlement, be unseated now, in the name of Jesus (Isaiah 47:1-5)

16. Every wicked altar monitoring and manipulating my marriage, I tear you down by fire and the blood of Jesus, in Jesus name (1 Kings 13:1-5; Matthew 3:10)

17. Ungodly curses and covenants flowing from my bloodline and my wife/husband's bloodline working against our marriage break by the blood of Jesus, in the name of Jesus (Numbers 23:23, 8)

18. I pour the blood of Jesus into the spring of my life and marriage for healing and restoration, in the name of Jesus (Revelations 12:11; Hebrews 12:24)

19. Anything in me working against my marriage and destiny, I identify and expel you, in Jesus name (Matthew 153; Psalm 18:44-45)

20. Any name the devil has called me, which God did not originally call me, I reject and denounce you by fire, in the name of Jesus (Colossians 2:14)

21. Favor beyond territorial boundaries, locate and distinguish me in my marriage and destiny, in the name of Jesus (Isaiah 46:11; Psalm 102:13)

22. Favor that cannot be resisted or denied, be released upon my life and marriage, in the name of Jesus (Genesis 50:20; Psalm 106:4-5)

23. Every area of incomplete deliverance in my life, my husband's life and marriage, receive complete deliverance by fire, in Jesus name (Isaiah 10:27)

24. Every witchcraft burial done against my marital glory and testimony, I cancel you and exhume my marital virtue by the blood of Jesus, in the name of Jesus (Nahum 1:13; 1 Samuel 30:8)

25. Every crazy pattern of attack that has kept me in the same spot, I dash you against the wall of fire, in the name of Jesus (Psalm 137:8-9)

26. Whatever the enemy has said will be impossible concerning my marriage, become divinely possible by the mercies of the Most High God, in the name of Jesus (Matthew 19:26; Luke 1:37)

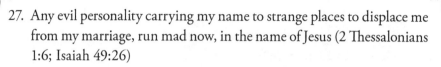

27. Any evil personality carrying my name to strange places to displace me from my marriage, run mad now, in the name of Jesus (2 Thessalonians 1:6; Isaiah 49:26)

28. Any marine initiations or dedications working against my marriage and settlement, break and release me by fire, in Jesus name (Colossians 2:14)

29. Any spirit husband/wife manipulating and fighting against my marriage, be disgraced and destroyed by fire, in the name of Jesus (Hebrews 12:29)

30. Marine witchcraft chains making it difficult for me to make progress in marriage and life, be shattered to pieces now, in the name of Jesus (Isaiah 54:15)

31. I walk out of my mother/father and I command my mother/father to walk out of me, in the name of Jesus (Genesis 27:40 KJV)

32. Any demonic marriage ceremony that was used to join me to any spiritual entity in marriage, I annul and dissolve you by the blood of Jesus, in the name of Jesus (Job 5:12; 1Peter 2:24)

33. Foundational witchcraft lockbox used to cage my marriage, be crushed and shattered by fire, in the name of Jesus (Isaiah 49:24-26)

34. I set on fire any marriage certificates, rings, clothes or other artifacts symbolizing my marriage to any spirit husband/wife, in the name of Jesus (Hebrews 12:29)

35. Any demonic incisions being used to manipulate my marital destiny, I neutralize your power by the blood of Jesus, in Jesus name (Colossians 2:14; Revelations 12:11)

36. Every serpentine hold over the glory and stability of my marriage, break and release me completely, in the name of Jesus (Isaiah 10:27)

37. I use the sword of fire of the Holy Ghost to cut off the head of the ancestral python terrorizing my marriage and destiny, in the name of Jesus (Isaiah 27:1)

38. You the powers of the waters, vomit my marital glory and virtues, in the name of Jesus (Job 20:15)

39. Any ancient python that has swallowed good things belonging to my spouse and I, vomit them by fire, in the name of Jesus (Joel 2:25-27)

40. Any marine power claiming any form of marriage to me, I divorce you, in the name of Jesus (Philippians 2:9-11)

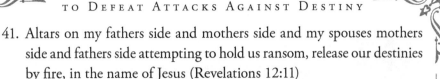
41. Altars on my fathers side and mothers side and my spouses mothers side and fathers side attempting to hold us ransom, release our destinies by fire, in the name of Jesus (Revelations 12:11)

42. Any blood covenant working against my marriage and life, be broken by the blood of Jesus, in the name of Jesus (Revelations 12:11; Hebrews 12:29)

43. Whatever has been used to turn my spouse against me, be reversed by the blood of Jesus, in the name of Jesus (Isaiah 7:5-7)

44. Covenants entered into with the sun, moon and stars against my marriage and destiny, fail and backfire, in Jesus name (Galatians 3:13)

45. Agreements entered into with the earth against my marriage, I overturn you by the power in the name of Jesus, in Jesus name (Isaiah 10:27; Nahum 1:13)

46. Holy Spirit, the heart of every man and woman is in your hand, so turn my spouses heart back to me in love and agreement, in the name of Jesus (Proverbs 21:1)

47. Any enchantment embarked upon to bring confusion and division between my spouse and I, be undermined and reversed by the blood of Jesus, in Jesus name (Numbers 23:23)

48. Sacrifices carried out with human or animal blood against my marriage and destiny, fail and backfire by the blood of Jesus, in Jesus name (Isaiah 54:17)

49. Let the wind of favor, prosperity and positive change begin to blow to the advantage of my marriage and destiny, in the name of Jesus (Psalm 102:13)

50. Finger of God, unseat the stubborn enemy of my marriage and destiny, and establish me for good, in the name of Jesus (Exodus 8:16-19)

51. I thank You Lord for testimonies and cover myself and my marriage with the blood of Jesus (Psalm 105:1-3)

Striking The Horse And The Rider

Scripture Reading: Zechariah 12:4, 1 John 3:8; Luke 10:19; 2 Timothy 4:18

Memory Verse/Confession: Proverbs 21:31

> *"The horse is prepared for the day of battle, but deliverance is of the LORD."*

Explanation:

Just as 'the preparations of the heart belong to man, but the answer of the tongue is from the LORD' (Proverbs 16:1), any horse and rider may arise, but the success of their enterprise is futile without God's approval. We know God is for us, therefore every horse and rider that has risen or shall rise against us will fall to his or her demise and shame, in Jesus name.

THEME: ASSOCIATE YOURSELVES AND BE BROKEN IN PIECES

1. Every power working with another to attack my destiny, I attack and crush you both, in Jesus name (Isaiah 43:16-17)
2. Hand of God that does valiantly, unsettle and tip over every horse and its rider assigned against my progress, in Jesus name. (Jeremiah 51:21-24)
3. Blood of Jesus, overcome the terror of every horse and its rider waging war against me, in Jesus name. (Zechariah 12:4)

4. I disappoint the devices of every enabler enabling attacks against my progress, in the name of Jesus (Job 5:12-13)

5. Any evil trigger programmed to trigger attacks against my fruitfulness, I dismantle you by the blood of Jesus (Ecclesiastes 10:8)

6. Every evil flight taken against me, crash-land instantly, in Jesus name (Psalm 9:15; 2 Thessalonians 1:6)

7. Any wicked mission collectively undertaken for my sake, fail and backfire tragically, in Jesus name (Isaiah 8:9-10 KJV)

8. I confuse and derail every ungodly journey undertaken to derail my prosperity, in Jesus name (Isaiah 19:1-3)

9. Let everyone visiting strange altars against me, receive judgment with such altars, in Jesus name. (Ezekiel 6:3-5; Deuteronomy 7:22-25; Isaiah 45:16)

10. Every horse and rider on a demonic mission against my destiny, receive divine disgrace and be confounded, in Jesus name (Isaiah 41:11-13; Zechariah 10:5)

Neutralizing The Power Of Satanic Weapons And Arrows

<u>Scripture Reading</u>: Isaiah 54:17; Psalm 91:1-8; Psalm 144:1; Isaiah 48:17; Exodus 15:3

<u>Memory Verse/Confession</u>: Ezekiel 39:9-10

> *"Then those who dwell in the cities of Israel will go out and set on fire and burn the weapons, both the shields and bucklers, the bows and arrows, the javelins and spears; and they will make fires with them for seven years. They will not take wood from the field nor cut down any from the forests, because they will make fires with the weapons; and they will plunder those who plundered them, and pillage those who pillaged them," says the Lord GOD.*

<u>Explanation</u>:

God declares that no weapon formed against you shall prosper, and every tongue raised against you qualifies for condemnation at your command (Isaiah 54:17). It is therefore within your authority to destroy all weapons of the enemy assigned against your peace; for our Lord Jesus has said the gates of hell shall not prevail against His church, and the truth is we are the church (Matthew 16:18). Take time to prayerfully war with these prayers, for the victory is already yours.

THEME: DEMOLISHING THE WEAPONS OF THE ENEMY

1. Every arrow of wickedness fired against my destiny, I quench you with the shield of faith and defeat you by the power in the blood of Jesus, in the name of Jesus (Psalm 91:5-6; Ephesians 6:16)

2. Every career-related arrow fashioned against my promotion, wither by fire, in Jesus name (Psalm 75:6-7; Nahum 1:13)

3. Every weapon of disagreement, separation and divorce, released against my marriage, locate your sender for destruction, in Jesus name (Psalm 144:6-8)

4. Household and family arrows affecting my ability to breakthrough, self-destruct, in the name of Jesus (Psalm 76:1-3; Zechariah 9:14-16)

5. Satanic deposits in my system resulting from arrows fired at me in my dreams, melt and be flushed out by the blood of Jesus. (Mathew 15:13; I John 1:7)

6. Physical poisons in my body as a result of arrows fired through polluted food, melt and be flushed out by fire, in Jesus name (Psalm 18:44-45; Hebrews 12:28-29)

7. Every ungodly covenant sponsoring evil arrows against me at designated periods of time, break and release me instantly, in Jesus name (Galatians 3:13; Isaiah 28:18)

8. You my body, receive the power to resist and deflect demonic arrows, in the name of Jesus (Ephesians 6:16, Isaiah 59:17)

9. Holy Spirit, turn my destiny into hot coals of fire, too hot for any wicked arrows, in Jesus name (Zechariah 2:5)

10. I release my potential and blessings from the spells and bewitchment of satanic arrows, in the name of Jesus (Numbers 23:23; Isaiah 10:27)

11. Arrow of the Most High God, locate and pull down every wicked altar sponsoring satanic arrows against my destiny, in the name of Jesus (Psalm 64:1-7, 2 Samuel 22:14-15)

Breaking The Yoke Of Oppression And Terror

<u>Scripture Reading</u>: Isaiah 54:14; Ecclesiastes 7:7; Micah 7:8; Psalm 9:9; Proverbs 14:31

<u>Memory Verse/Confession</u>: Psalm 35:1-8

> *"Plead my cause, O LORD, with those who strive with me; fight against those who fight against me. Take hold of shield and buckler, and stand up for my help. Also draw out the spear, and stop those who pursue me. Say to my soul, "I am your salvation." Let those be put to shame and brought to dishonor who seek after my life; let those be turned back and brought to confusion who plot my hurt. Let them be like chaff before the wind, and let the angel of the LORD chase them. Let their way be dark and slippery, and let the angel of the LORD pursue them. For without cause they have hidden their net for me in a pit, which they have dug without cause for my life. Let destruction come upon him unexpectedly, and let his net that he has hidden catch himself; into that very destruction let him fall."*

<u>Explanation</u>:

"…Into that very destruction let him fall," says King David. Any oppression against your life, into that very oppression will your enemies fall. Any terror against your life, into that very terror will they fall. Its fire for fire.

THEME: FIRE FOR FIRE

1. Every reign of terror established against my life, disintegrate completely, in the name of Jesus (2 Timothy 4:18; Psalm 34:18; Psalm 72:4)

2. Any power that oppressed my parents that is oppressing my life, I bind you and render you powerless, in the name of Jesus. (1 John 4:4; Psalm 11:3; Obadiah 1:17; Matthew 18:18)

3. Burden lifting anointing of the Holy Spirit, lift every burden upon my life, in Jesus name (Psalm 55:22; Psalm 118:5-7; Isaiah 10:27)

4. Yoke breaking anointing of the Holy Ghost, break every yoke of wickedness in my life, in the name of Jesus (Isaiah 10:27-NLT; Nahum 1:13; Galatians 5:1)

5. Light of Christ, attack any darkness in any department of my life, in the name of Jesus (Psalm 18:28-29; John 1:4-5)

6. Every power terrorizing me in my dreams, receive the terror of the Lord, in the name of Jesus. (2 Chronicles 1:6; Proverbs 11:8; Ephesians 6:10-18)

7. Any pattern of oppression being used against me, break and release me by fire, in the name of Jesus (Colossians 1:13-14, John 8:36)

8. I receive the shoes of fire and I trample upon every serpent and scorpion of affliction attacking my destiny, in the name of Jesus (Luke 10:19; Zechariah 7:10)

9. Every cloud of oppression blocking my sun of glory, I dislodge you by thunder, in the name of Jesus. (Jude 1:9, Psalm 121:6-8)

10. I receive the anointing that cannot be insulted or cursed, in the name of Jesus (1 John 4:4; 1 John 5:18)

Silencing The Voice Of The Goliath Of Your Life

Scripture Reading: 1 Samuel 17:20-52; 2 Chronicles 32:1-16; Lamentations 3:37

Memory Verse/Confession: Exodus 15:3

"The Lord is a man of war; the Lord is His name"

Explanation:

The spirit of Goliath represents those problems, challenges and enemies that have become seemingly impossible to overcome. You must realize the Lord is always ahead of your problems and situations. Anytime there is a Goliath terrorizing your life, there is always a David waiting in the shadows to bring him down. Just as David used the sword of his enemy to decapitate him forever, so will your enemies' own weapon turn against them. As the Lord assured Joshua, so He also assures you, that 'He will never leave you nor forsake you' (Joshua 1:5).

THEME: LET MY DAVID ARISE, AND
MY GOLIATH BE WASTED!

1. Every goliath specially anointed to bring me down, I locate your forehead with the stones of fire, in the name of Jesus (1 Samuel 17:8-11, 16, 32-51)
2. Powers that are boasting against my present and future, run mad and be wasted, in Jesus name (2 Kings 19:10-14, 35-37; Psalm 37:15)

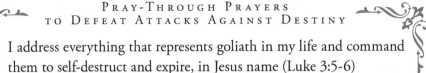
3. I address everything that represents goliath in my life and command them to self-destruct and expire, in Jesus name (Luke 3:5-6)

4. Let every wicked finger writing against my life be condemned and wither by fire, in the name of Jesus (Isaiah 41:11-12)

5. I challenge and erase every ungodly and destructive writing against my destiny, by the power in the blood of Jesus (Colossians 2:14; Revelations 12:11)

6. Holy Spirit, multiply tribulation in the life of all those troubling my destiny, in Jesus name (2 Thessalonians 1:6; Revelations 13:10)

7. I silence every stubborn voice from hell, speaking against my progression, in Jesus name (Lamentations 3:37; Isaiah 54:17)

8. Every wicked goliath prophesying against my wellbeing, I silence you permanently by the power in the name of Jesus (Proverbs 18:10)

9. Blood of Jesus, overturn every evil cry against me, and begin to speak better things as it concerns my life and destiny, in Jesus name (Hebrews 12:24)

10. Any foundational goliath that has refused to let me go, I crush your head with the hammer of the Word of God, in the name of Jesus (Jeremiah 23:29)

11. Every serpentine goliath making life difficult for me, I receive the shoes of iron and fire, and trample you to death, in the name of Jesus (Luke 10:19)

12. Goliath in my household conniving with other goliaths on the outside to attack my destiny, receive disgrace by fire, in the name of Jesus (Matthew 10:36; Isaiah 31:3)

13. Any goliath living and crawling within my body, I strangle and emasculate you by fire, in the name of Jesus (Hebrews 12:29)

Pharaoh Must Expire

<u>Scripture Reading</u>: Exodus 14:1-31, Isaiah 19:1-3; Exodus 9:1-35; Exodus 4:22-23

<u>Memory Verse/Confession</u>: 2 Chronicles 7:14

> *"If my people who are called by my name will humble themselves and pray and seek my face and turn from their wicked ways, then I will hear from heaven, and will forgive their sin and heal their land"*

<u>Explanation</u>:

One of the primary missions and ministries of our Lord Jesus Christ was to set the captive free (Luke 4:18). This is why 1 John 3:8B clearly states, "For this purpose the Son of God was manifested, that He might destroy the works of the devil." Therefore you should not be suffering under any yoke of oppression when Christ has set you free; for the Scriptures declare that who the Son has set free, is free indeed (John 8:36).

THEME: DELIVERANCE FROM THE YOKE OF THE OPPRESSOR

1. Every power of Pharaoh and his army pursuing my destiny, perish in your own Red Sea in Jesus name (Exodus 14:28)
2. Pharaoh of household witchcraft operating against my destiny, be extinguished by fire in Jesus name (Matthew 10:36; Isaiah 49:25)

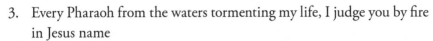

3. Every Pharaoh from the waters tormenting my life, I judge you by fire in Jesus name

4. (Exodus 7:4; Exodus 12:12)

5. You the unrepentant strongman of the night attacking me in my dreams, I arrest you by fire in Jesus name (Matthew 13:25; Luke 11:21-22)

6. Any stubborn power sitting on the throne of my destiny, I unseat you by fire in Jesus name (Isaiah 47:1)

7. I decree confusion in the camp of Pharaoh and the oppressors, in Jesus name (Exodus 14:24-25)

8. Every occult witchcraft initiation and dedication working against my destiny, release me instantly in Jesus name (Isaiah 10:27)

9. Pharaoh of ancestral curses and covenants holding my life down, I break loose from you in Jesus name (Galatians 3:13-14; Colossians 2:14)

10. Let every weapon and power of Pharaoh being used to torment me turn against him and his army, in Jesus name (Revelations 13:10; 1 Thessalonians 1:6; Psalm 37:14-15)

11. I trample upon every serpent and scorpion of Pharaoh, in Jesus name (Luke 10:19)

12. You the power of Pharaoh harassing my life, the blood of Jesus is against you, in the name of Jesus (Revelations 12:11; 1 John 3:8B)

13. I repossess double of everything Pharaoh and his oppressors have stolen from me, in the name of Jesus (Isaiah 61:7; 1Samuel 30:8)

14. I decree that every Pharaoh and slave master I have encountered in the past, I will see them no more, in the name of Jesus (Exodus 14:13-14)

15. Lord, I thank you for answered prayers and testimonies, in Jesus name (1 Thessalonians 5:18, Psalm 100:4)

Dispersing and Scattering Evil Gatherings Against Your Wellbeing

Scripture Reading: Isaiah 8:9-10; Acts 23:12-22; 2 Corinthians 11:32-33

Memory Verse/Confession: Isaiah 54:15

> *"Indeed they shall surely assemble, but not because of Me. Whoever assembles against you shall fall for your sake."*

Explanation:

God is against ungodly gatherings, especially when they are against His children. Therefore, every gathering not of God, He monitors closely. And if those gatherings are against you, they shall surely scatter, says the Lord of hosts!

THEME: DESTROYING EVIL GATHERINGS

1. Every ungodly gathering against me, scatter never to re-gather again, in the name of Jesus (Isaiah 8:9-10-KJV)
2. I confuse and dismantle every ungodly agreement sponsored against me, in Jesus name (Psalm 18:37-46)
3. Any wicked congregation assembled against me, fall for my sake, in the name of Jesus (Deuteronomy 28:7)
4. I release confusion and panic into the camp of my enemies, in the name of Jesus (Psalm 35:4-6; Exodus 14:24-25)
5. Angels of the Most High God, gather against every gathering assembled against me, in the name of Jesus (Hebrews 1:14; 2 Kings 19:35)

6. I confuse the unity of every contrary agreement working against me, in the name of Jesus (Judges 7:19-25)

7. Fire of the Most High God, scatter and disintegrate every conscious union against my peace, in Jesus name (Hebrews 12:29)

8. I silence every united voice of contention opposing my progress, in the name of Jesus (Psalm 35:1; Isaiah 54:17)

9. Let everything causing my enemies to agree against me begin to make them disagree amongst themselves, in the name of Jesus (2 Kings 3:20-24)

10. My Father and My God, confuse every oracle of the wicked sponsoring evil agreements and gatherings against me and my household, in Jesus name (Isaiah 19:1-3)

Pushing The Wicked Into Their Own Traps
(Fire For Fire)

Scripture Reading: Psalm 57:6; Psalm 35:1-28; Psalm 18:1-50; Isaiah 54:15

Memory Verse/Confession: Proverbs 11:8

> *"The righteous is delivered from trouble, and it comes to the wicked instead."*

Explanation:

These prayers should reinforce what you already know, and may teach you what you something new. The chief priests and Jews probably thought Calvary and the tomb would trap Jesus forever, but they were mistaken, for He is free. The trap they set for Him was ineffective, and so is every trap that is set for you. We do know that the wicked have no peace (Isaiah 48:22), and so believe that any trap set against your peace and joy shall trap those who set it, and you will pass by free, as the Psalmist declares, "Let the wicked fall into their own nets, while I escape safely," (Psalm 141:10).

THEME: RETURN TO SENDER

1. Every trap the wicked have prepared for my steps, may they fall into it themselves, in the name of Jesus (Psalm 35:7-8)
2. Any door of affliction opened for my sake, be closed in the face of your openers, in Jesus name (Revelations 3:7)
3. Financial traps set against me, catch your owners, in the name of Jesus (Proverbs 11:8)

4. Every power trying to lead me into captivity, go into divine captivity, in Jesus name (Ephesians 4:8; Revelations 13:10)

5. Any friendly enemy secretly setting traps to entrap me, fall into your own traps, in the name of Jesus (Psalm 55:9-15)

6. Holy Spirit, expose and dismantle every trap erected against my success, in the name of Jesus (Daniel 2:22; Job 5:12)

7. Every unfriendly friend planning to entrap me with my words, I implicate you by your words, in Jesus name (Psalm 9:15-16; Isaiah 8:10)

8. Any trap of the wicked currently holding me in bondage, release me and entrap your owners, in Jesus name (Psalm 124:7)

9. O Lord, visit the wickedness of the wicked upon their heads and multiply it, in the name of Jesus (2 Thessalonians 1:6)

10. Let every ambush against me in my home, place of work, ministry or marriage, backfire by fire, in the name of Jesus (Isaiah 54:15; Acts 23:11-35)

11. I break and frustrate every pattern of collective betrayal I have been experiencing from childhood, in Jesus name (Isaiah 8:9-10 KJV; Isaiah 31:3)

Arresting Spiritual and Physical Thieves

Scripture Reading: John 10:10; Exodus 22:2-4; John 12:1-6-NIV; Proverbs 6:30-31

Memory Verse/Confession: Job 20:15

> *"He swallows down riches and vomits them up again; God casts them out of his belly."*

Explanation:

The Bible reveals that the mission of the enemy is to steal, kill and to destroy, but our Lord Jesus came to give us life, and life more abundantly (John 10:10). God wants you to have live in abundance. Gods Word also promises a sevenfold return for what the enemy has stolen (Proverbs 6:30-31), but this is small when compared to abundant life. It's your time to be restored.

THEME: I PURSUE, OVERTAKE, AND RECOVER ALL!

1. Dream criminal stealing from me in my dreams, I arrest and retrieve all you've stolen from me, in the name of Jesus (Matthew 13:25)
2. Every ministry of Judas assigned to deplete my finances, I frustrate you by the blood of Jesus, in Jesus name (John 12:3-6; Job 5:12)
3. Strange money introduced into my finances to steal from me, I attack and render you powerless by the blood of Jesus, in Jesus name (Leviticus 10:1-2; Revelations 12:11)

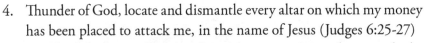

4. Thunder of God, locate and dismantle every altar on which my money has been placed to attack me, in the name of Jesus (Judges 6:25-27)

5. Angels of the Living God, break into every satanic warehouse and take back by force everything the enemy has stolen from me, in the name of Jesus (Luke 11:21-22; Micah 2:13)

6. Fisher Angels of the Most High God, go into every body of water and marine habitation, and begin to fish out everything the marine kingdom has stolen from me, in the name of Jesus (Jeremiah 16:16)

7. Hunter Angels of the Living God, go into every spiritual realm of darkness and begin to hunt down everything that has been stolen from me, in Jesus name (Jeremiah 16:16)

8. Anything programmed into my life to steal from me, I identify and suffocate you by fire, in the name of Jesus (Isaiah 7:5-7)

9. O Lord, turn my life and blessings and finances to hot coals of fire; too hot for any spiritual or physical thief to handle, in the name of Jesus (Malachi 3:11; Hebrews 12:29)

10. Financial demons assigned to terrorize my financial destiny, I command you to go into captivity for my sake, in Jesus name (Revelations 13:10; Ephesians 4:8)

11. Father Lord, I ask for forgiveness if I have in any way robbed you in tithe and offering, thereby allowing the devourer access to me; I pray that you convict my heart to always give you the first fruit of my increase in Jesus name (Malachi 3:8-10)

Casting Down Evil Imaginations

Scripture Reading: 2 Corinthians 10:3-6; Proverbs 23:7A; Proverbs 4:23; Romans 12:2

Memory Verse/Confession: Proverbs 19:21

> "There are many plans in a man's heart, nevertheless the LORD's counsel—that will stand."

Explanation:

Paul admonishes us to cast down every imagination, and bring them to the obedience of Christ (2 Corinthians 10:3-6). That means whatever thoughts you have that are not in line with the Word of God must be brought under submission to what God says. For example, God says by the stripes of Jesus you were healed (1 Peter 2:24). You're already healed since the payment has been made for whatever sickness the devil may bring your way. As such, it does not matter what your mind is telling you concerning a body part, an illness or a diagnosis. God's Word prevails, and will prevail in your life.

THEME: I RECEIVE THE MIND OF CHRIST

1. Every wicked imagination working against my advancement, I cast you down, in the name of Jesus (2 Corinthians 10:4-5)
2. Any thought or imagination that does not line up with God's Word must fail in my life, in the name of Jesus (Nahum 1:9-10 - KJV)
3. Every evil device conceived in any mind against my wellbeing, be frustrated and fail, in the name of Jesus (Job 5:12)

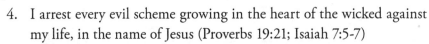

4. I arrest every evil scheme growing in the heart of the wicked against my life, in the name of Jesus (Proverbs 19:21; Isaiah 7:5-7)

5. Let every imagination and thoughts of witchcraft against me, backfire by fire, in the name of Jesus (Genesis 6:5; Isaiah 54:17)

6. I command failure for every evil plan in the heart of anyone against my progress, in the name of Jesus (Isaiah 44:24-25 - KJV)

7. Every ungodly counsel flowing from evil desires operating against me, I render you null and void, in the name of Jesus (Isaiah 8:9-10 - KJV)

8. Holy Spirit, confuse and disappoint every imagination of darkness influencing my life, in the name of Jesus (Acts 12:7-11; Proverbs 14:19)

9. Blood of Jesus, erase the handwritings of the record of evil thoughts and imaginations speaking against me, in the name of Jesus (Colossians 2:14; Hebrews 12:24)

10. I am not for cursing, so I decree myself 'uncursable', in the name of Jesus (Numbers 23:7-8; Galatians 3:13)

11. I am for blessing, so I declare myself blessed, in the name of Jesus (Genesis 12:3; Numbers 24:10)

12. I declare that I am not double-minded, but have the mind of Christ, in the name of Jesus (James 1:8; Philippians 2:5, 18)

Destroying the Works of the Devil

Scripture Reading: 1 John 3:8B; Matthew 15:13; Isaiah 10:27; Isaiah 49:24-26; Psalm 91:1-16

Memory Verse/Confession: Colossians 1:13

> *"He has delivered us from the power of darkness and conveyed us into the kingdom of the Son of His love."*

Explanation:

God has given you the authority of His Son Jesus Christ (Luke 10:19), by His Spirit, which resides in you, and has commanded you to 'occupy till He returns' (John 20:21; Luke 19:13-KJV). Also, whatever you bind on earth according to His will is bound in Heaven, and whatever you loose on earth according to God's will is also loosed in Heaven (Matthew 18:18). We have been commanded to destroy the works of the devil, and as sons and daughters of Light, darkness cannot overcome us (John 1:5).

THEME: EVERY KNEE MUST BOW

1. Every plot of hell, programmed against my life, I destroy you instantly, in the name of Jesus (Job 5:12)
2. Finger of God, identify and destroy every finger of hell fighting against my destiny, in the name of Jesus (Exodus 8:16-19A)
3. Serpent of the Most High God, swallow the serpent of every pharaoh that has refused to let me go, in the name of Jesus (Exodus 7:8-12)

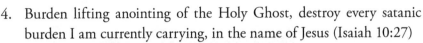
4. Burden lifting anointing of the Holy Ghost, destroy every satanic burden I am currently carrying, in the name of Jesus (Isaiah 10:27)

5. Yoke breaking anointing of the Holy Spirit, demolish every yoke of the wicked hindering my life, in the name of Jesus (Nahum 1:13)

6. Blood of Jesus, silence every voice of oppression speaking contrary to my liberty, in the name of Jesus (Hebrews 12:24; 2 Corinthians 3:17)

7. I receive divine strength to break loose from every chain of stagnancy holding me back, in the name of Jesus (Genesis 27:40)

8. I dismantle and pull down every pillar supporting bondage in my life, in the name of Jesus (Jeremiah 1:10; Judges 6:25-27)

9. I lift up the standard of the Holy Spirit against every flood of the devil assigned against my rising up, in the name of Jesus (Isaiah 59:19; Isaiah 40:28-31)

10. Every knee of wickedness attempting to prevent my progress, bow completely, in the name of Jesus (Isaiah 45:23; Philippians 2:9-11)

Dealing With Unfriendly Friends

<u>Scripture Reading</u>: Job 16:19-21; Psalm 146:3-5; Proverbs 21:1; Genesis 50:20

<u>Memory Verse/Confession</u>: 2 Samuel 15:31

> *"Now someone told David, saying, "Ahithophel is among the conspirators with Absalom." And David said, "O LORD, I pray, make the counsel of Ahithophel foolishness."*

<u>Explanation</u>:

No man can offer you what only God can give. This is why the Bible tells us that 'Cursed is the man who puts his trust in man and makes flesh his strength" (Jeremiah 17:5); because we are to love our fellowman, but put our absolute trust in God. A friend can be a complete blessing or an absolute foe. So discernment is needed to choose your friends wisely. May the Lord open your eyes as you pray these prayers.

THEME: IDENTIFYING AND CUTTING TIES WITH BAD FRIENDS

1. Holy Spirit, expose and disgrace every unfriendly friend, secretly or openly attacking my destiny, in Jesus name (Deuteronomy 29:29; Psalm 41:9-11; Isaiah 44:26-KJV)
2. Anyone I call my friend, who heaven calls my enemy, manifest your true color, and receive divine disgrace, in Jesus name (Psalm 35:1-8; Samuel 15:31)

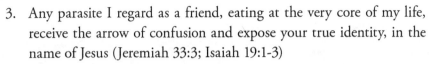
3. Any parasite I regard as a friend, eating at the very core of my life, receive the arrow of confusion and expose your true identity, in the name of Jesus (Jeremiah 33:3; Isaiah 19:1-3)

4. Unfriendly relationships, sucking the milk of my life dry, vomit everything you've swallowed and be rendered powerless, in Jesus name (Job 20:15; Job 5:12)

5. Any green snake hiding under the green grass of my hospitality to attack me, I receive the shoes of iron and fire, and trample their serpents and scorpions to death, in Jesus name (Luke 10:19)

6. O Lord, withdraw your favor and goodness from anyone I have been good to, paying me back evil for good, in the name of Jesus (Proverbs 17:13)

7. I release shame and reproach upon every enemy pretending to be my friend, who is secretly attacking my destiny, in the name of Jesus (Jeremiah 20:10-11)

8. Father Lord, restore to me everything I have lost to unfriendly relationship, in the name of Jesus (Joel 2:25-27; Psalm 41:9)

9. Every congregation of wicked and unfriendly friends gathered against my prosperity, scatter for my sake, in the name of Jesus (Isaiah 54:15; Isaiah 8:9-10-KJV)

10. Friends that have benefited from my benevolence presently speaking and working against me, go into captivity for my sake, in the name of Jesus (Psalm 41:9-11; 2 Thessalonians 1:6)

11. Dear Lord, thank you for wisdom and discernment regarding every relationship in my life, and help me to seek you about all my friendships, in Jesus name (James 1:5; 1 Timothy 2:1)

Lord Show My Enemies A Token of Your Power

<u>Scripture Reading</u>: Colossians 2:15; Exodus 14:24-31; Psalm 84:11; Matthew 3:10

<u>Memory Verse/Confession</u>: Romans 9:17

> *"For the Scripture says to the Pharaoh, "For this very purpose*
> *I have raised you up, that I may show My power in you, and*
> *that My name may be declared in all the earth."*

<u>Explanation</u>:

God in His wisdom raised up Pharaoh to reveal His power. There is nothing the Lord is not aware of; and at times, a storm may be to showcase His glory and power in the battles we face. "And Moses said to the people, "Do not be afraid. Stand still, and see the salvation of the LORD, which He will accomplish for you today. For the Egyptians whom you see today, you shall see again no more forever. The LORD will fight for you, and you shall hold your peace" (Exodus 14:13-14). Be still and know He is God (Psalm 46:10A).

THEME: GOD OF VENGEANCE

1. Thunder of God, locate the hiding place of my secret enemies for exposure and disgrace, in Jesus name (Luke 8:17; 2 Samuel 22:14-15)
2. Light of God, blow the cover of my hidden enemies, in the name of Jesus (Daniel 2:22)

3. Terror of the Most High God, terrorize every troubler of my Israel, in the name of Jesus (Zephaniah 3:19; 1 Kings 18:17-18)

4. Thunderbolt from heaven, locate and scatter unto desolation every gathering of the wicked against my destiny, in Jesus name (Nahum 1:12-13-NIV)

5. By the power in the name of Jesus, I command every power harassing my destiny to go into generational bondage, in Jesus name (Exodus 17:14-16; Isaiah 60:14)

6. Blood of Jesus, confuse and render useless every instrument of attack my enemies are using against me, in the name of Jesus (Revelations 12:11; Exodus 12:13)

7. Lord of hosts, move against every army of the wicked advancing against me, in the name of Jesus (Isaiah 49:25B-26)

8. O Lord, show my enemies a token of your power to break their hold over my destiny, in Jesus name (Psalm 18:13-14; Isaiah 59:19)

9. East wind of God, blow back every wind of affliction programmed against my success, in the name of Jesus (Exodus 14:21)

10. Man of war, enter into battle with every foundational power attacking my destiny, in the name of Jesus (Exodus 15:3; Psalm 35:1-10)

11. O Lord, show my unrepentant stubborn pursuers who the real Boss is, in the name of Jesus (Deuteronomy 32:39; 1 Samuel 2:6)

12. Heavenly Father, every way in which I may have offended you and opened the door for my enemies, cleanse me now according to Your Word (1 John 1:9)

The Overcoming Blood

<u>Scripture Reading</u>: Revelations 12:11; Hebrews 12:24; 1 Peter 2:24; Hebrews 9:22

<u>Memory Verse/Confession</u>: Exodus 12:13

> *"Now the blood shall be a sign for you on the houses where you are. And when I see the blood, I will pass over you; and the plague shall not be on you to destroy you when I strike the land of Egypt."*

<u>Explanation</u>:

The Blood of Jesus is a speaking blood speaking mercy on our behalf. That's why it is said to speak better things than the blood of Abel, whose blood sought revenge for his murder (Genesis 4:1-10). Because the blood of redemption is speaking over us, we must boldly declare that which Christ did for us on the Cross of Calvary, assured that by the words of our testimonies we are able to overcome the wicked one.

THEME: THE SPEAKING AND OVERCOMING BLOOD

1. Blood of Jesus, emasculate every unrepentant stubborn pursuer of my destiny, in the name of Jesus (Colossians 2:15; Romans 3:25)
2. Blood of the Lamb of God, mark my enemies and their source of strength for instant destruction, in the name of Jesus (Exodus 12:13)

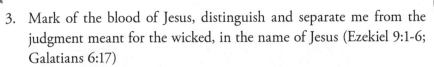

3. Mark of the blood of Jesus, distinguish and separate me from the judgment meant for the wicked, in the name of Jesus (Ezekiel 9:1-6; Galatians 6:17)

4. Let the power in the blood overcome on my behalf, but be the very weapon for the destruction of my stubborn enemies and problems, in the name of Jesus (Revelations 12:11)

5. Better speaking power in the blood of Jesus, begin to announce me in every palace I have been ordained to rule over, in the name of Jesus (Hebrews 12:24)

6. Favor in the blood of Jesus, turn the hearts of kings and queens to favor and promote me, in the name of Jesus (Daniel 2:20-21; Proverbs 21:1; Isaiah 60:10-11)

7. Blood of Jesus, promote me above and beyond the power of animal and human sacrifices negatively affecting me, in the name of Jesus (Colossians 2:14; Hebrews 12:24)

8. Mercy in the blood of the Lamb, deliver me from the consequences of generational curses and cleanse my bloodline from every evil inheritance, in the name of Jesus (Galatians 3:13; Hebrews 9:22)

9. Demonic spiritual marks placed upon me to hinder my advancement, be erased by the authority in the blood of Jesus, in the name of Jesus (Deuteronomy 15:12-17; Colossians 2:14)

10. Polluted foundational garments which the devil is using to resist my progress, be removed by reason of the sacrifice of the Blood and broken Body of our Lord Jesus Christ, in the name of Jesus (Zachariah 3:1-5)

11. Dear Lord, thank You for giving me power to speak life over my destiny, in Jesus name (Proverbs 18:21)

Crushing The Head of the Oppressor

<u>Scripture Reading</u>: Romans 16:20; Isaiah 27:1; Job 20:15; Psalm 33:25-27 KJV

<u>Memory Verse/Confession</u>: Luke 10:19

> *"Behold, I give you the authority to trample on serpents and scorpions, and over all the power of the enemy, and nothing shall by any means hurt you."*

<u>Explanation</u>:

The Sword of the Spirit is the Word of God (Ephesians 6:17). Equipped with this in your hand or mouth per se, you will crush the head of any oppressor, be it sickness, fear or whatever the case may be. Your warfare is based on the Scriptures, and Christ came to set us free giving us access to freedom (Galatians 5:1). Heaven is backing you up and you are victorious in this war!

THEME: BRUISING THE HEAD OF THE ENEMY

1. I receive the shoes of iron and fire, and I crush the head of leviathan, in the name of Jesus (Isaiah 27:1; Deuteronomy 33:25-27-KJV)
2. Father Lord, sit upon the head of my wicked enemies for maximum damage, in the name of Jesus (Isaiah 40:22)
3. King of Kings, trample upon and crush the heads of my stubborn and unrepentant enemies and suffocate them, in the name of Jesus (Isaiah 66:1A; Psalm 2:1-5)

4. I fire the arrow of insanity into the heads of my cruel and wicked enemies holding me in bondage and command them to run mad, in the name of Jesus (Isaiah 44:24-25 - KJV)

5. Father Lord, confuse every imagination of my enemies assigned to undermine my safety, in the name of Jesus (Proverbs 19:21; Psalm 55:1-9 - NIV)

6. Every thought of wickedness programmed against my destiny, I cast you down by fire, in the name of Jesus (2 Corinthians 10:3-6)

7. I dash the head of every strongman attacking me against the wall of fire, in the name of Jesus (Luke 11:21-22)

8. I use the head of my stubborn pursuers and enemies as a stepping stone into my land of breakthrough, in the name of Jesus (Joshua 1:3; 2 Thessalonians 1:6)

9. I take back by force, everything oppressors have stolen from me, in the name of Jesus (Job 20:15; 1 Samuel 30:8)

10. I stand upon the chest of the goliath of my destiny and I use his sword to cut off his head, in the name of Jesus (1 Samuel 17:48-51; Revelations 13:10)

11. Father, I ask you to cleanse me of all sin and iniquity that may have caused my enemies to prevail against me in the past (Joshua 7:11-12)

Confusing The Tongues of The Wicked

Scripture Reading: Genesis 11:1-19; Isaiah 19:1-5; Hebrews 12:24; John 1:1-5

Memory Verse/Confession: Psalm 55:9

> *"Destroy, O Lord, and divide their tongues, for I have seen violence and strife in the city."*

Explanation:

God's Word declares, 'Who is he who speaks and it comes to pass, when the Lord has not commanded it?'(Lamentations 3:37). 'What can man do to me?' David asks in Psalm 56:11. In other words, there is nothing that can happen to you without the Lord's permission or knowledge. The truth is 'You are more than a conqueror through Him who loved you' (Romans 8:37). Your life has already changed as you believe and pray these prayers!

THEME: DESTROYING THE AGENDA OF EVIL TONGUES

1. I confuse the minds and tongues of every ungodly army gathered against my life, in the name of Jesus (Isaiah 54:15; Isaiah 8:9-10-KJV)
2. Every confession that does not agree with God's word concerning my destiny, fail completely, in Jesus name (Isaiah 54:17B)
3. Any voice of dissent contending with my blessings, I render you dumb, in the name of Jesus (Lamentations 3:37)
4. O Lord, deliver and hide me from the slander of tongues, in the name of Jesus (Job 5:21; Psalm 59:1-8)

5. Father Lord, turn every counsel of the wicked against me to foolishness, in the name of Jesus (2 Samuel 15:31)

6. My Father and My God, bless everyone who blesses me and curse everyone who curses me, in the name of Jesus (Genesis 12:3)

7. Holy Spirit, anoint my tongue for signs, wonders and miracles, in the name of Jesus (Isaiah 8:18; Proverbs 18:20)

8. O Lord, make my tongue an instrument for blessing, in the name of Jesus (Job 22:27-28; Proverbs 18:21)

9. Any ancestral altar speaking against my moving forward, be silenced by fire, in the name of Jesus (Galatians 3:13; Colossians 2:14; 2 Corinthians 5:17)

10. I revoke and reverse every prayer or prophecy issued against my destiny, in the name of Jesus (Job 5:12; Lamentations 3:37)

11. Father forgive me for using my tongue as a weapon instead of an instrument to praise You and pray for others (Psalm 34:1; James 3:6)

The Law Of Retribution

<u>Scripture Reading</u>: Proverbs 14:19; 2 Thessalonians 1:6; Exodus 20:5-6; Romans 12:19

<u>Memory Verse/Confession</u>: Psalm 9:15-16,

> *"The nations have sunk down in the pit which they made; in the net which they hid, their own foot is caught. The LORD is known by the judgment He executes; the wicked is snared in the work of his own hands."*

<u>Explanation</u>:

Our God is a God of retribution, who repays in full (Jeremiah 51:56 - NIV), and has His Angels encamp around those who fear Him (Psalm 34:7). God will pay in full every evil brought upon His children by the enemy (Romans 12:19). This is why the Scriptures declare, "The Lord is a Man of war, the Lord is His name" (Exodus 15:3).

THEME: VISITING THE DEEDS OF THE WICKED UPON THEM

1. Let deliverance begin to come forth from every place of bondage and captivity in my life, in the name of Jesus (Romans 5:20B)
2. I receive power to trample upon the wicked and their snares, in the name of Jesus (Luke 10:19; Isaiah 41:15-16)
3. Father Lord, judge and give the wicked a taste of their wickedness, in the name of Jesus (Ezekiel 18:20; Psalm 7:9-10)

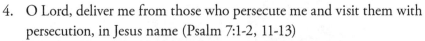
4. O Lord, deliver me from those who persecute me and visit them with persecution, in Jesus name (Psalm 7:1-2, 11-13)

5. Father Lord, push my detractors into every pit they have dug for my soul, in the name of Jesus (Psalm 7:15-16)

6. Every net prepared for me due to envy and jealousy, catch and destroy your owners, in Jesus name (Psalm 35:7-9; Job 34:11)

7. Holy Spirit, pour upon me the anointing that cannot be ensnared, in the name of Jesus (Mark 16:17-18)

8. Every plan to trap or implicate me, fail and backfire now, in the name of Jesus (Proverbs 19:21; Psalm 57:6)

9. I convert and use every trap the enemy has set for me as steps to my breakthroughs, in the name of Jesus (Romans 8:28; Genesis 50:20)

10. I use the lifeless bodies of my unrepentant stubborn pursuers as a ladder to climb to my place of rest, in the name of Jesus (1 Samuel 17:48-51)

Releasing Confusion Among Your Enemies

<u>Scripture Reading</u>: Judges 7:19-25; Genesis 1:1-3; John 5:1-5; Exodus 14:24-29

<u>Memory Verse/Confession</u>: Isaiah 41:11

> *"Behold, all those who were incensed against you shall be ashamed and disgraced; they shall be as nothing, and those who strive with you shall perish."*

<u>Explanation</u>:

Confusion puts a person in a state of distress and restlessness, so they are not able to function effectively. May your prayers confuse and scatter every plot, scheme and conspiracy against your peace.

THEME: RELEASING DISTRESS & RESTLESSNESS INTO THE CAMP OF THE ENEMY

1. I convert the blood of Jesus into a virus and introduce it into the computer of the enemy, in the name of Jesus (Revelations 12:11)
2. Let everything making my enemies agree against me begin to make them disagree, in the name of Jesus (Isaiah 19:1-3)
3. O Lord, confuse the language and tongues of my enemies, in the name of Jesus (Genesis 11:1-9)
4. Father Lord, give my stubborn pursuers a useless assignment that will keep them permanently away from my affairs, in the name of Jesus (Isaiah 3:11)

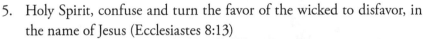
5. Holy Spirit, confuse and turn the favor of the wicked to disfavor, in the name of Jesus (Ecclesiastes 8:13)

6. I confuse everything currently working to the advantage of my enemies and command that they begin to work against them, in the name of Jesus (Proverbs 11:8)

7. Lord Jesus, introduce confusion into the unity of my household enemies, in the name of Jesus (Isaiah 54:15)

8. Father Lord, turn my affairs into hot coals of fire, too hot for any enemy to attack or confuse, in the name of Jesus (Hebrews 12:29; Zechariah 2:8-9)

9. Let the anointing of confusion and disagreement prevail in the camp of my detractors, in the name of Jesus (Exodus 14:24-28)

10. I command nature and all of God's creation to begin to work for the downfall of my contenders, in the name of Jesus (Judges 5:20-21)

Taking The Battle To The Camp Of The Enemy

<u>Scripture Reading</u>: Psalm 3:1-8; Psalm 18:37-42; Genesis 22:17; Genesis 24:60

<u>Memory Verse/Confession</u>: 2 Thessalonians 1:6

> *"Since it is a righteous thing with God to repay with tribulation those who trouble you"*

<u>Explanation</u>:

Our God is a man of war (Exodus 15:3), who trains us in the act of battle and warfare (Psalm 144:1; Psalm 18:34), so we're equipped for every conceivable situation. Know for certain that whatever God allows the enemy to bring your way, he has prepared and equipped you before hand for it, and you're able to bear and overcome it in His wisdom and strength.

THEME: ATTACKING AND TERRORIZING YOUR ATTACKERS

1. I send the fire of judgment upon every evil unity of the enemy assigned against our lives and testimony in Jesus name (Isaiah 7:5-7)
2. Any man or woman that have entered into dangerous covenants against me and my family, fail and destroy yourself, in Jesus name (Acts 23:12-24)
3. Evil powers of my mother and fathers house that have been sitting upon the throne of my destiny, I unseat you permanently, in the name of Jesus (Isaiah 47:1-5)

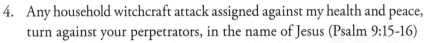

4. Any household witchcraft attack assigned against my health and peace, turn against your perpetrators, in the name of Jesus (Psalm 9:15-16)

5. Any attack of serpentine powers assigned to paralyze my finances and prosperity, backfire by fire, in the name of Jesus (Isaiah Luke 10:19; Psalm 57:6)

6. I decree instant confusion and restlessness upon every unrepentant stubborn pursuer of my career, business or ministry, in the name of Jesus (Isaiah 19:1-5)

7. I write the obituary of every wicked power in charge of my case in the name of Jesus (Psalm 35:1-8; Revelations 13:10)

8. Every satanic grave digger digging graves for me and my family, be pushed into your own grave and buried alive, in the name of Jesus (Psalm 118:17; Proverbs 11:8)

9. Every unrepentant troubler of my destiny and family, I send you to an early grave, in Jesus name (2 Thessalonians 1:6; Psalm 18:37-38)

10. Every conscious or unconscious evil covenant or dedication to the powers of the waters affecting me, break and release us by fire, in Jesus name (Isaiah 10:27; Obadiah 1:17)

11. I jump out of every circle and cage of evil family curses and patterns, in the name of Jesus (Galatians 3:13)

12. I reject and reverse every evil clinical prophecy and diagnoses given to me by the doctors, in the name of Jesus (Lamentations 3:37; Matthew 18:18)

13. Every ungodly covenant entered into by witchcraft and marine witchcraft powers against my family and I, be rendered impotent, in the name of Jesus (Colossians 2:14)

14. Every power that has sworn that over their dead body will I prosper and excel, expire instantly, in the name of Jesus (Genesis 12:3)

15. Blood of Jesus, speak deliverance, healing, and resurrection concerning my body and life, in the name of Jesus (Hebrews 12:24)

16. O Lord, keep covenant with me as the Great Deliverer and Man of war concerning my family's health in Jesus name (Numbers 10:9; Exodus 15:3)

17. Any satanic personality responsible for delaying and stagnating my life, be exposed, disgraced and carry your evil load, in Jesus name (Ezekiel 12:21-28-KJV)

Ry

18. I claim divine and miraculous intervention concerning my situation, in the name of Jesus (Matthew 19:26; Luke 1:37)
19. I decree I, my spouse and my children will not die, but we shall live and declare the works of the Lord in the land of the living, in Jesus name (Psalm 118:17; Psalm 91:16)
20. I claim deliverance and restoration as it concerns me and my family, in Jesus name
21. I and my family are blessed and we will testify of Your goodness in the land of the living, in Jesus name (Deuteronomy 28:1-14)
22. I cover my family and I with the blood of Jesus, and decree there shall be no re-enforcement, re-gathering, or re-attacking of the enemy as a result of these prayers, in Jesus name (Revelations 12:11)

Divine Protection

Scripture Reading: Psalm 91:1-16; Psalm 27:1-6; Revelations 12:7-11; Isaiah 49:24-26; Isaiah 18:44-45; Psalm 20:1-8

Memory Verse/Confession: Psalms 91:1-2

> *"He who dwells in the shelter of the Most High will abide in the shadow of the Almighty. I will say to the LORD, "My refuge and my fortress, my God, in whom I trust."*

Explanation:

The Lord is a Shelter and Protector (Psalm 121:1-8). His passion for our safety and protection is so much that the Bible calls us the apple of His eye (Zechariah 2:8). As a man would on impulse crush or deflect anything that attempts to penetrate or interfere with the apple of his eye, so the Lord watches over us with protection.

THEME: THE NAME OF THE LORD IS A STRONG TOWER

1. Let every conspiracy against my life, be exposed, frustrated, and backfire, in Jesus name (Acts 20:2-3)
2. O Lord, disappoint every expectation of the wicked concerning my life, in the name of Jesus (Acts 12:11)
3. Blood of Jesus, expose and disgrace every plan of the wicked targeted against me, in the name of Jesus (Acts 23:12-24)
4. Father Lord, enter into battle with any ungodly congregation gathered against my destiny, in the name of Jesus (Isaiah 54:15)

5. Any evil cooperation targeted to cripple my destiny, I frustrate and judge you, in the name of Jesus (Psalm 140:1-5)

6. You powers of the wicked that are out to kill me, receive the arrow of confusion and destroy yourself, in the name of Jesus (Psalm 26:1-5; Revelations 13:10)

7. I shall not die but live to a ripe old age, to declare the works of the Lord in the land of the living, in the name of Jesus (Psalm 118:17)

8. I run into the name of the Lord and I am safe, in the name of Jesus (Proverbs 18:10)

9. I prophesy upon my life that I will prosper and attain God's best for my life, in the name of Jesus (Deuteronomy 28:1-14)

10. I access the secret place of the Most High and I abide under the shadow of the Almighty, in the name of Jesus (Psalm 91:1)

11. O Lord, deliver me from the power of every word spoken against me under demonic authority, in the name of Jesus (Job 5:21; Lamentations 3:37)

12. Father Lord, let the fire of Your protection be upon me and my household, in the name of Jesus (Zechariah 2:5)

13. In Your faithfulness O Lord, establish and guard me against the evil one, in the name of Jesus (2 Thessalonians 3:3)

14. O Lord, You are my God and My Rock, defend your investment in my life, in the name of Jesus (2 Samuel 22:3-4 - KJV)

15. Lord Jesus, all authority belongs to You, protect and preserve me from the evil of the wicked, in the name of Jesus (Matthew 28:18)

16. Father Lord, protect me and my household from the wrath of my enemies, in the name of Jesus (Psalm 138:7)

17. My Lord and My God, preserve me from all evil and prosper me in the midst of my enemies, in the name of Jesus (Psalm 121:7-8; Psalm 23:5)

18. I cover myself with the blood of Jesus and envelope my destiny with the fire of the Holy Ghost, in Jesus name (Revelations 12:11; Hebrews 12:29)

19. I decree there shall be no re-enforcement, re-grouping, or re-attacking against me as a result of these prayers, in Jesus name (Isaiah 7:5-7; Isaiah 54:17)

Destroying The Power Of Curses

<u>Scripture Reading</u>: Joshua 6:26; 1 Kings 16:34; 2 Kings 2:19-22

<u>Memory Verse/Confession</u>: Galatians 3:13

> *"Christ has redeemed us from the curse of the law, having become a curse for us (for it is written, "Cursed is everyone who hangs on a tree")."*

<u>Explanation</u>:

Curses are pronouncements that provoke supernatural powers to work against the wellbeing of an individual. Our Lord and Savior Jesus Christ paid the supreme price for our liberation from the power of curses. Our words and prayers spoken under the anointing of the Word of God are filled with authority to nullify and neutralize curses. What we are trying to explain is that Christ took upon Himself every curse possible on the Cross of Calvary, thereby delivering us from the power of curses. And the fact that He is no longer on that tree, but alive and well; you also should therefore be alive and well, because of His sacrifice.

THEME: BLESSED BEYOND THE CURSE

1. I break every curse of unprofitable hard work hovering over my life, in the name of Jesus (Deuteronomy 30:19)
2. Blood of Jesus, destroy every curse connected to my bloodline, in the name of Jesus (Revelations 12:11; Hebrews 12:24)

3. Every curse that affected my father and mother, which is currently affecting my life, break and release me by fire, in Jesus name (Psalm 11:3; Ezekiel 18:20)

4. Any word spoken against me under demonic authority, I neutralize you by the authority of God's Word, in the name of Jesus (Isaiah 54:17)

5. Ancestral curses working against my destiny, be broken by the blood of Jesus (Leviticus 26:39-42; Galatians 3:13-14)

6. Every curse relating to my place of birth affecting my life, be broken by the blood of Jesus (Revelations 21:11; Isaiah 10:27)

7. I am blessed beyond the curse therefore I declare myself uncursable, in the name of Jesus (2 Corinthians 5:17; Romans 8:2)

8. The Word of God says 'He who blesses me is blessed and he who curses me is cursed,' therefore I trouble every troubler of my Israel, in the name of Jesus (Genesis 12:3; 1 Kings 18:17-18; Revelations 13:10)

9. I am not for cursing but for blessings, I therefore claim blessings and reject curses, in Jesus name (Deuteronomy 11:26-28; Deuteronomy 30:19; Matthew 18:18)

10. Generational curses hovering over my life and family, break and release me by fire, in the name of Jesus (Colossians 2:14; Obadiah 1:17)

11. Household witchcraft curses spoken against my fruitfulness, fail and backfire now, in the name of Jesus (Lamentations 3:37-38; Isaiah 54:17)

12. Occult pronouncements and declarations working against my health and wellbeing, I overturn and neutralize you by the authority of the Word of God, in the name of Jesus (Isaiah 59:19; Numbers 23:23)

13. Father, I repent of every sin and iniquity allowing the enemy access into my life, in Jesus name (Psalm 51:1-2)

Breaking Cycles of Adversity

<u>Scripture Reading</u>: 2 Corinthians 4:8-9 (NLT); Philippians 4:12-13; 1 Peter 5:10; Proverbs 24:10

<u>Memory Verse/Confession</u>: Isaiah 54:17 (KJV)

> *"No weapon that is formed against thee shall prosper; and every tongue that shall rise against thee in judgment thou shalt condemn. This is the heritage of the servants of the LORD, and their righteousness is of me, saith the LORD."*

<u>Explanation</u>:

The Bible reveals that in this world we will have troubles (John 16:33), so trials and adversity are a fact of life; but Jesus encourages us to cheer up, because He has overcome the world and has become our peace.

THEME: DESTROYING PATTERNS OF RE-OCCURING ADVERSITY

1. O Lord, identify and arrest every agent of affliction, working against my destiny, in Jesus name (1 Peter 5:8-9A; 2 Corinthians 4:8-9)
2. I break free from the hold of any power sponsoring adversity in my life, in the name of Jesus (Genesis 27:40 – KJV)
3. Father Lord, bring adversity upon every instrument of adversity warring against my destiny, in the name of Jesus (Psalm 57:6)
4. Traps of adversity set for me and my family, miss your target and locate your owners, in the name of Jesus (Psalm 35:1-9)

5. I release divine judgment upon every alter of adversity assigned against my life, in the name of Jesus (Judges 6:25-27)

6. Let every horse and it's rider pursuing my destiny, drown in their own Red Sea, in the name of Jesus (Isaiah 31:3; Exodus 15:20-21)

7. Adversity flowing from my household enemies, I arrest and disband you, in the name of Jesus (Matthew 10:36; Isaiah 54:15)

8. Doors of affliction through which the enemy has been accessing my life, be shut completely, in the name of Jesus (Nahum 1:9; Matthew 18:18)

9. Every voice of adversity that has risen up against me, be silenced forever, in the name of Jesus (Isaiah 54:17B; Lamentations 3:37)

10. Weapons of adversity employed to afflict me spiritually and physically, be roasted and melt by fire, in the name of Jesus (Psalm 68:1-2)

11. Attacks of adversity directed against my health and fitness, be broken by instantly, in the name of Jesus (Proverbs 14:19; Job 5:12)

12. I sit upon and crush the head of every stubborn spirit of adversity that has refused to leave me alone, in the name of Jesus (2 Thessalonians 1:6)

13. Heavenly Father, I repent of any sin in my life that has allowed adversity in my life, in Jesus name (Psalm 51:1-2)

Neutralizing the Spirit of Astrology

<u>Scripture Reading</u>: Deuteronomy 18:9-12; Daniel 4:7; Deuteronomy 4:19; Deuteronomy 17:2-5

<u>Memory Verse/Confession</u>: Ephesians 6:12 (NASB)

> *"For our struggle is not against flesh and blood, but against the rulers, against the powers, against the world forces of this darkness, against the spiritual forces of wickedness in the heavenly places."*

<u>Explanation</u>:

Astrology is the study and possible worship of the host of heaven, and is also one of the tools used by the devil to deceive and hold many people in captivity. Many individuals have been led astray and deceived into venturing into this abomination, and a lot of destinies have been entangled in this practice, and caged or destroyed. These prayers are designed to provide deliverance, healing and restoration to those who have fallen victim to this demonic practice.

THEME: BREAKING FREE FROM THE POWERS OF ASTROLOGY

1. Heavenly Father, I repent of any consultation with astrologers, tarot cards or psychics, and ask forgiveness for any reading of horoscopes in past, in the name of Jesus (Psalm 51:1-19)

2. I close any doors I may have opened by my involvement with astrology, in Jesus name (Leviticus 19:31; Ecclesiastes 10:8)

3. I nullify and bring to naught every counsel of the astrologers regarding my life, in Jesus name (Daniel 4:7; Isaiah 8:10 – KJV)

4. I curse and decree divine judgment on all false gods of astrology, in Jesus name (Jeremiah 10:11)

5. Father Lord, confuse and neutralize the counsel of anyone manipulating the stars against me, in Jesus name (Isaiah 19:1-4)

6. Let the finger of God move against every power enforcing the evil works of astrology against me, in the name of Jesus (Exodus 8:16-19)

7. Father Lord, deliver and release my destiny from the hold of the spirit of astrology, in the name of Jesus (Psalm 50:15)

8. O Lord, destroy every alter of astrology that has been raised up against me, in the name of Jesus (Isaiah 59:19; Judges 6:25-27)

9. Every work of astrology being used to manipulate my destiny, be destroyed by the blood of Jesus, in the name of Jesus (1 John 3:8B; 1 Samuel 28:3-15)

10. My Lord and My God, confuse and scatter every collective voice of astrology speaking against my wellbeing, in the name of Jesus (Genesis 11:1-9)

11. Powers invoking the sun, the moon and the stars against me, perish with your enchantments, in the name of Jesus (Numbers 23:23; Exodus 22:18 - KJV)

12. Anyone petitioning the queen of heaven against me, I judge you and your beggarly queen by fire, in the name of Jesus (Jeremiah 44:15-27; Jeremiah 10:11)

13. Satanic personalities worshipping the starry heavens in order to undermine my glory, fail and be disgraced, in the name of Jesus (Psalm 35:1-9)

14. Any psychic being consulted to destroy my destiny, perish with the one consulting you, in the name of Jesus (Revelations 13:10; 2 Thessalonians 1:6)

15. Anyone practicing clairvoyance to derail me from God's chosen path for my blessing, repent or perish, in the name of Jesus (Exodus 22:18 – KJV)

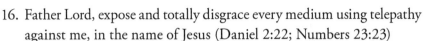
16. Father Lord, expose and totally disgrace every medium using telepathy against me, in the name of Jesus (Daniel 2:22; Numbers 23:23)

17. Any man or woman chanting my name before the powers of the sun and moon to harm me, receive the harm intended for me, in the name of Jesus (Proverbs 11:8; Proverbs 14:19; Proverbs 19:21)

18. Blood of Jesus, answer on my behalf when my spirit is summoned through astrology, in the name of Jesus (Hebrews 12:24)

19. I cover myself with the blood of Jesus and envelope myself with the fire of the Holy Ghost, in the name of Jesus (Revelations 12:11; Hebrews 12:29)

Destroying The Foundation & Walls of Satanic Prisons

Scripture Reading: Acts 16:19-40; John 10:10; Isaiah 10:27; Psalm 18:44-45

Memory Verse/Confession: Isaiah 10:27

> *"It shall come to pass in that day that his burden will be taken away from your shoulder, and his yoke from your neck, and the yoke will be destroyed because of the anointing oil."*

Explanation:

The sacrifice of Christ broke every foundation of bondage and established the standard for salvation and liberty for humankind. Nothing can alter or change this truth. Once this revelation is received, believed and acted upon through prayer and in obedience to the will and Word of God, victory is sure.

THEME: PULLING DOWN EVIL FOUNDATIONS THAT IMPEDE FREEDOM

1. Earthquake of the Most High God, shake down the foundation of every satanic prison in my life, in the name of Jesus (Isaiah 31:3; Nahum 1:13)
2. Bulldozer of the Holy Ghost, identify and bulldoze every altar supporting bondage in my life, in the name of Jesus (Micah 2:13; Isaiah 19:1-4)
3. Altars of my father's house and altars of my mother's house caging my destiny, I pull you down by fire, in the name of Jesus (Judges 6:25-27)

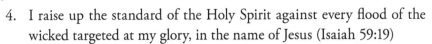
4. I raise up the standard of the Holy Spirit against every flood of the wicked targeted at my glory, in the name of Jesus (Isaiah 59:19)

5. Let praise begin to pull down the foundation of every prison that prayer alone has not been able to pull down in my life, in the name of Jesus (Psalm 22:2-3 - NLT; 2 Chronicles 20:22-23 - NLT)

6. I command prayer to begin to pull down the foundation of every prison praise is not able to pull down in my life, in the name of Jesus (Job 22:27-30)

7. Let my offering and tithes begin to pull down the foundation of every satanic prison prayer and praise are not able to pull down in my life, in the name of Jesus (Psalm 50:5; Malachi 3:8-12; Luke 6:38)

8. I shake-loose and dismantle every satanic foundation enforcing wicked covenants and curses against me, in the name of Jesus (Galatians 3:13; Romans 8:1)

9. Every evil handwriting empowering satanic prisons in my foundation and life, I blot out and render you null and void, by the power in the blood of Jesus (Colossians 2:14; Revelations 12:11)

10. Animal and human blood sacrifices empowering satanic prisons and bondages in my life, I revoke and silence you by the blood of Jesus, in the name of Jesus (Hebrews 9:22; 1 John 3:8B)

11. Wicked foundational altars speaking against liberty in my life, I silence you completely, in the name of Jesus (Hebrews 12:24; Lamentations 3:37)

Overcoming Powers That Humiliate And Embarrass You
(Overcoming Powers That Make You Thresh Wheat In The Winepress)

<u>Scripture Reading</u>: Judges 6:1-16; Genesis 3:10; Isaiah 50:7; Mark 8:38; Hebrews 12:1-2

<u>Memory Verse/Confession</u>: Isaiah 61:7

> *"Instead of your shame you shall have double honor, and instead of confusion they shall rejoice in their portion. Therefore in their land they shall possess double; everlasting joy shall be theirs."*

<u>Explanation</u>:

Romans 9:33 reads, "As it is written: 'Behold, I lay in Zion a stumbling stone and rock of offense, and whoever believes in Him will not be put to shame" (NKJV). The underlying factor behind this Scripture is that Jesus is a stumbling Stone that will make men stumble, a Rock that will make them fall, but those that trust and believe in Him shall not be put to shame. This is very comforting and reassuring.

THEME: FROM SHAME TO FAME

1. Any power assigned to constantly embarrass me, receive divine and permanent disgrace, in the name of Jesus (Revelations 13:10 - KJV)

2. I release myself and my family from every covenant of disgrace my ancestors have entered into, in the name of Jesus (2 Corinthians 5:17; Galatians 3:13)

3. Holy Spirit, deliver me from every foundational confusion making me to put square pegs in round holes and round pegs in square holes, in the name of Jesus (Psalm 11:3; Psalm 50:15)

4. I refuse to thresh wheat in the winepress and crush grapes in the threshing floor, in the name of Jesus (1 Corinthians 14:33)

5. O Lord, help me to be at the right place, at the right time, doing the right thing for the right reasons, in the name of Jesus (Romans 8:14; Psalm 37:4; Matthew 7:7-8)

6. Holy Spirit, grant me insight and direction for success in all my endeavors, in the name of Jesus (Deuteronomy 29:29; Isaiah 30:21)

7. I fire back to sender, every arrow of shame assigned against my destiny, in the name of Jesus (Proverbs 11:8)

8. I refuse to be put to shame; rather, I move from shame to fame, in the name of Jesus (Psalm 25:3; Isaiah 49:23-24)

9. Any pattern of embarrassment prevalent in my family, I am not your candidate, in the name of Jesus (Psalm 25:1-3)

10. Every gathering assembled to humiliate me, scatter completely never to gather again, in the name of Jesus (Isaiah 54:15)

11. Any attack targeted to make me look incompetent and bad, be instantly exposed and disgraced, in the name of Jesus (Isaiah 41:11-13)

12. Statements and publications intended to embarrass and humiliate me, be rendered ineffective by the blood of Jesus (Hebrews 12:24; Isaiah 54:17B)

13. I receive double honor for every shame and disgrace I have ever suffered, in the name of Jesus (Isaiah 61:7)

Destroying The Spirit Of Witchcraft

Scripture Reading: 1 Samuel 15:23; Psalm 14:1-4; Leviticus 19:31; Deuteronomy 18:9-12

Memory Verse/Confession: Leviticus 19:26 (AMP)

> *"You shall not eat anything with the blood; neither shall you use magic, omens, or witchcraft (or predict events by horoscope or signs and lucky days)."*

Explanation:

Witchcraft manipulates. It changes the natural course of a thing, in that, it attempts to move whatever it's trying to manipulate in a direction other than it's God-ordained path. These prayers are designed to help us resist or altogether destroy the influence and menace of witchcraft. Say no to this age long tool of the devil by aggressively praying these prayers.

THEME: ARRESTING THE SPIRIT OF ENCHANTMENT

1. I decree that surely there is no enchantment against me, neither is there divination against my family, in the name of Jesus (Numbers 23:23)
2. In agreement with the Word of God, I decree death to every spirit of witchcraft attacking my destiny and wellbeing, in the name of Jesus (Exodus 22:18)
3. Every voice of bewitchment speaking against my wellbeing, I silence and render you powerless, in the name of Jesus (Isaiah 54:17B; Hebrews 12:24)

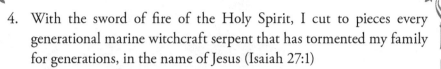
4. With the sword of fire of the Holy Spirit, I cut to pieces every generational marine witchcraft serpent that has tormented my family for generations, in the name of Jesus (Isaiah 27:1)

5. I identify and uproot every witchcraft plantation in my body, in the name of Jesus (Matthew 15:13)

6. Axe of Holy Ghost, locate the root of every tree of bewitchment in my destiny and cut them down, in the name of Jesus (Luke 3:9)

7. Night and early morning caterers repeatedly feeding me with poison in my dreams, I force-feed you with your evil food, in the name of Jesus (Isaiah 49:26)

8. Fire of God, melt and render ineffective every witchcraft deposit in my life, in the name of Jesus (Hebrews 12:29)

9. I receive the anointing that cannot be 'bewitched' and declare myself 'unenchantable', in the name of Jesus (Mark 16:17-18)

10. Any spirit husband or wife coming to pollute me sexually in my dreams, I roast you with fire today, in the name of Jesus (2 Thessalonians 1:6)

11. Blood of Jesus, neutralize and flush out every witchcraft poison in my body, in the name of Jesus (Psalm 18:44-45)

12. I receive the shoes of iron and fire and I trample upon every serpent and scorpion of witchcraft assigned against my destiny, in the name of Jesus (Luke 10:19)

13. Any witchcraft entity pressing me down in my sleep, receive divine disgrace, in the name of Jesus (Isaiah 49:24-25)

14. Witchcraft scratches and marks inflicted on me in my sleep, be neutralized and erased by the blood of Jesus (Matthew 13:25; Psalm 129:3-4)

15. I command every foundational witchcraft python to vomit all of my goodness they have swallowed, in the name of Jesus (Job 20:15)

Inquiry & Revelation Prayer

Scripture Reading: Daniel 2:22; Psalm 25:14; Jeremiah 33:3; Matthew 16:17; Hebrews 1:1

Memory Verse/Confession: Deuteronomy 29:29

> *"The secret things belong to the Lord our God, but the things revealed belong to us and to our children forever, that we may follow all the words of this law."*

Explanation:

God is an all-knowing God. Nothing is hidden from His all-seeing eyes. He is the keeper and revealer of secrets (Deuteronomy 29:29); and He will reveal His secrets to those who fear and obey Him (Psalm 25:14). In fact, the Bible says God does nothing without revealing it to His servants the Prophets (Amos 3:7; Ephesians 3:5). May the Lord open your spiritual eyes and ears as you pray.

THEME: THE REVEALER OF SECRETS

1. Father Lord, I thank you for my life, in the name of Jesus (Psalm 103:1-5)
2. Holy Spirit, reveal to me the secret behind my life, in the name of Jesus (Deuteronomy 29:29)
3. O Lord, show me clearly who I am spiritually, in the name of Jesus (Jeremiah 33:3)

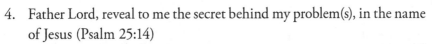
4. Father Lord, reveal to me the secret behind my problem(s), in the name of Jesus (Psalm 25:14)

5. Lord Jesus, expose and show me in clear terms, the deep and dark covenants and agreements affecting my life negatively, in the name of Jesus (Matthew 7:7-8; Luke 12:2-3)

6. Holy Spirit, take me into my subconscious and expose by revelation the root of my challenges, in the name of Jesus (Proverbs 8:17)

7. My Father and My Lord, reveal to me the foundational altars on father and mother's side, opposing my destiny, in the name of Jesus (Judges 6:25-27)

8. Father Lord, anoint my spiritual eyes and ears to see and hear beyond the physical into the supernatural, in the name of Jesus (2 Kings 6:8-20)

9. Holy Spirit, expose and disgrace every unfriendly friend secretly working against my advancement, in the name of Jesus (1 Corinthians 2:10; John 2:24-25)

10. Lord Jesus, show me clearly what the hidden issues of my life are, in the name of Jesus (Proverbs 25:2)

11. O Lord, reveal to me my spiritual gifts and what you have called me to do in Your Kingdom, in Jesus name (John 15:15)

12. Father Lord, expose and consume with Your fire all the little foxes clogging my spiritual eyes and ears, in the name of Jesus (Songs of Solomon 2:15)

13. Lord Jesus, show me in clear terms who my household enemies are, in the name of Jesus (Matthew 10:36)

14. Lord I thank you for answered prayers and great testimonies, in Jesus name (Psalm 20:1-8)

Defeating Attacks Against Destiny

Scripture Reading: Psalm 35:1-29; Psalm 23:1-6; Psalm 271-14; Psalm 91:1-16

Memory Verse/Confession: 2 Timothy 4:18

> *"And the Lord will deliver me from every evil work and preserve me for His heavenly Kingdom. To Him be glory forever and ever. Amen!"*

Explanation:

Our Lord is a God that specializes in disappointing and defeating the works of the enemy. This is why Job 5:12 (KJV) states clearly that, "He disappoints the devices of the crafty, so that their hands cannot perform their enterprise." Whether it's a plan within their hearts (Proverbs 19:21), or they are trying to implement any of their wicked plans (Proverbs 14:19; Isaiah 59:19); God is ahead of our enemies.

THEME: BORN TO WIN, BORN TO REIGN

1. Anyone who has known me intimately, and has sworn to destroy me, destroy yourself, in the name of Jesus (Proverbs 11:8)
2. Any person who has benefitted from me and is trying attack me, receive the judgment of the fire of God, in the name of Jesus (Proverbs 17:13)

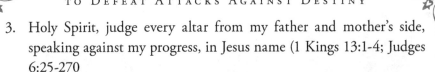

3. Holy Spirit, judge every altar from my father and mother's side, speaking against my progress, in Jesus name (1 Kings 13:1-4; Judges 6:25-270

4. Every ancestral serpentine covenant, warring against my destiny, break and release me now, in the name of Jesus (Isaiah 10:27; Isaiah 27:1)

5. Blood of Jesus and the liquid fire of the Holy Ghost, begin to melt and flush out every evil deposit in my system, in the name of Jesus

6. I cough out and vomit every poison and evil food eaten from the table of the enemy, in the name of Jesus (Matthew 13:25; Matthew 15:13)

7. Any man or woman investing in my downfall, perish in my place, in the name of Jesus (Revelations 13:10)

8. Any person who has lived with me in the past, using my weaknesses against me, be exposed and disgraced, in the name of Jesus (Psalm 109:1-20; Psalm 35:12-17)

9. Any power that has sworn that over their dead body will I live to old age, receive the arrow of sudden death, in Jesus name (Psalm 7:15-16; Psalm 57:6; 2 Thessalonians 1:6)

10. I will not die but live to a ripe old age, and declare the works of the Lord, in the land of the living, in the name of Jesus (Psalm 118:17; Psalm 91:16)

11. Fire of deliverance, begin to burn from the crown of my head to the soul of my feet, in the name of Jesus (Hebrews 12:29; Obadiah 1:17)

12. Favor of God, lift me up and distinguish me, in the name of Jesus (Psalm 102:13; Psalm 106:4-5)

13. Father, I thank you for answered prayer, and decree there shall be no re-enforcement or re-attacking against me, in the name of Jesus (Ecclesiastes 3:14)

Confusing The Oracle Of The Wicked

Scripture Reading: Isaiah 44:24-26 (KJV)

Memory Verse/Confession: Job 5:12 (KJV)

> *"He disappointeth the devices of the crafty, so that their hands cannot perform their enterprise."*

Explanation:

Confusion is a weapon the Lord regularly uses to undermine the efforts of the wicked against His sons and daughters. This can be described as a situation where the enemy's mental capacity is attacked to the extent that that they are no longer able to comprehend, understand, or make logical or rational decisions.

THEME: RECEIVE CONFUSION AND SELF-DESTRUCT

1. I confuse and disgrace every oracle being consulted for my sake, in the name of Jesus
   (Numbers 22:1-6)
2. Thou serpent of the Lord swallow the serpent of my pharaoh, in the name of Jesus
   (Exodus 7:8-12)
3. Every power controlling my destiny by divination, be paralyzed by fire, in Jesus name
   (Numbers 23:23; Exodus 22:18 - KJV)

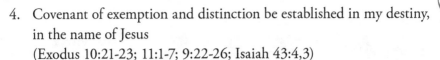
4. Covenant of exemption and distinction be established in my destiny, in the name of Jesus
   (Exodus 10:21-23; 11:1-7; 9:22-26; Isaiah 43:4,3)

5. Every altar or oracle with my name on it, scatter and burn to ashes, in the name of Jesus
   (Colossians 2:14; Isaiah 54:17)

6. Evil gatherings targeted against me and Gods goodness in my life, scatter never to reassembled, in Jesus name (Isaiah 54:15)

7. Let divine distress and confusion breakout in the camp of my unrepentant and stubborn pursuers and let them fight and destroy each other, in Jesus name (2 Chronicles 20:20-23; Isaiah 19:1-4)

8. Every satanic luggage placed upon my destiny, be uprooted and placed upon your sender now, in the name of Jesus(Proverbs 11:8)

9. Lord, visit my family strongman for judgment and death on the day his life is sweetest to him, in the name of Jesus (Luke 11:21-22)

10. Witchcraft soldiers assigned to attack my destiny, fight yourselves unto death, in the name of Jesus (2 Thessalonians 1:6)

11. Every witchcraft magnet attracting affliction to my life, be shattered by thunder, in the name of Jesus (1 Samuel 7:10; 2 Samuel 22:14-15)

I Refuse To Be A Victim

Scripture Reading: 2 Corinthians 22-27; 2 Corinthians 4:7-12; 2 Corinthians 5:21; 2 Timothy 3:12

Memory Verse/Confession: Job 3:25

> *"For the thing I greatly feared has come upon me, and what I dreaded has happened to me."*

Explanation:

Christ was victimized that we might be delivered from the claws of sin and death. And because Jesus has paid the price for our freedom, we no longer have to be victims of the harassment and lies of the enemy. The Word of God assures us that wherever the Spirit of God is there is liberty (2 Corinthians 3:17).

THEME: I WILL NOT BE VICTIMISED

1. Job 1:6-12
   a. O Lord, identify and disgrace every presence and work of the devil in my life and situation, in Jesus name
   b. Every conversation going on in the spiritual realm against my destiny, be confused and frustrated, in Jesus name
2. Job 1:7; 1 Peter 5:8; Revelations 12:10; 1 Peter 5:9
   a. As the enemy is seeking whom to devour, I declare my life is not its candidate, in the name of Jesus

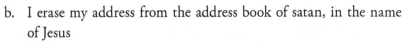
    b.   I erase my address from the address book of satan, in the name of Jesus

3. Job 5:12

    a.   Every attempt of the enemy to locate and attack me and my household, be frustrated, in the name of Jesus

    b.   Let every journey the devil has undertaken for my sake end in disappointment, in the name of Jesus

4. Job 1:9-11; Hebrews 12:24

    a.   Father Lord, re-enforce your edge of protection around me and my family, in the name of Jesus

    b.   Every power speaking against my prosperity, be silenced instantly by the blood of the Lamb, in the name of Jesus

5. Job 1:14-17; Revelations 12:11; John 10:10

    a.   Blood of Jesus defeat every battle the devil is waging against my prosperity and staff of bread, in the name of Jesus

    b.   Every gathering and conspiracy to steal, kill and destroy my destiny, scatter completely, in the name of Jesus

6. Job 1:18-19; Deuteronomy 4:24

    a.   Any power targeting my life, my spouse and children for destruction, die in our place, in the name of Jesus

    b.   Every book of tragedy in which my name and the name of my family members have been written for death, receive fire and be roasted, in the name of Jesus

7. Job 2:3-7; Job 22:27-28

    a.   I identify and frustrate every attack of the enemy against my health, in the name of Jesus

    b.   Powers targeting my body organs for sickness, you will not succeed, in the name of Jesus

8. Job 3:1-6

    a.   Father Lord, deliver me from any attack that will cause me grief and sorrow, in the name of Jesus

    b.   I reject anything that will make me reject and curse the day I was born, in the name of Jesus

    c.   Father Lord, do not allow me to experience any trial that will make me deny or doubt you, in the name of Jesus

9. Esther 3:8-11; Esther 7:9-10

   a. Holy Spirit, identify and crush all powers and satanic personalities that are ready to pay for my destruction, in the name of Jesus

   b. Let every ransom offered for my downfall be rejected, in the name of Jesus

   c. Father Lord, expose and disgrace any enemy desperate to eliminate me, in the name of Jesus

   d. Any gallows prepared to hang me, backfire and hang the one who prepared you, in the name of Jesus

10. Job 42:7; Genesis 13:8-9; Joshua 7:16-26

   a. O Lord, help me to identify and get rid of every Lot in my camp, in the name of Jesus

   b. Father Lord, expose and disgrace every congregation of unfriendly friends hanging around me, in the name of Jesus

   c. Every friendly enemy on assignment to betray and stab me in the back, receive divine destruction and perish, in the name of Jesus

   d. Any Achan in my camp inviting the wrath of God against me, be exposed and extinguished, in the name of Jesus

11. Job 42:10-16; Joel 2:25-27; Isaiah 61:7; 1 Samuel 30:8

   a. O Lord, grant me double blessing for my trouble, in the name of Jesus

   b. Father Lord, grant me double honor for my shame, in the name of Jesus

   c. I receive double restoration for everything I have lost, in the name of Jesus

   d. I pursue, overtake and recover everything the enemy has stolen from me, in the name of Jesus

   e. Holy Spirit, help me to continually forgive and pray for those who offend me, in the name of Jesus

Disgracing & Disbanding Wicked Gatherings Against My Destiny

Scripture Reading: Psalm 35:1-28; Psalm 91:1-16; 1 John 3:8B

Memory Verse/Confession: (i) Isaiah 54:15 (KJV)

> *"Behold, they shall surely gather together, but not by me: whosoever shall gather together against thee shall fall for thy sake."*

(ii) Isaiah 8:9-11 (KJV)

> *"Associate yourselves, O ye people, and ye shall be broken in pieces; and give ear, all ye of far countries: gird yourselves, and ye shall be broken in pieces; gird yourselves, and ye shall be broken in pieces. Take counsel together, and it shall come to nought; speak the word, and it shall not stand: for God is with us."*

Explanation:

God's Word tells us clearly that the enemy will surely gather, but he does not approve their gatherings. We also have a covenant assurance that they that gather against us will fall for our sake. The Scriptures are emphatic on the point that Christ is the head of principalities and powers, so we can be confident that the Lord closely monitors and can disappoint the outcome of the works of darkness.

THEME: I REFUSE TO BE AMBUSHED

1. Every evil expectation of the wicked assigned against my life, fail completely, in the name of Jesus (Acts 12:11)
2. Any strange fire projected against my destiny and peace, I put you out right now, in the name of Jesus (Leviticus 10:1-2; Hebrews 11:32-34)
3. Wicked covenants that have been entered into with the earth against me, I overturn them by the authority in the blood of Jesus, in the name of Jesus (Revelations 12:11; Colossians 2:14)
4. Agreements entered into with the elements (earth, wind and fire) against myself and my family, backfire by fire, in the name of Jesus (Galatians 3:13-14; 2 Thessalonians 1:6)
5. Whatever has been spoken into this land against me, I decree you will not prosper, in the name of Jesus (Lamentations 3:37)
6. Coffins and graves that have been prepared for me and my family, swallow your preparers instantly, in the name of Jesus (Proverbs 11:8; Revelations 13:10)
7. Any altar on my mother and fathers side that have been invoked to attack my finances, I pull you down and render you powerless, in the name of Jesus (Judges 6:25-27)
8. Every seat of witchcraft contending against God's goodness in my life and family, I set you ablaze, in the name of Jesus (Revelations 16:10-11)
9. Any household witchcraft conspiracy to harm or eliminate me and my children before our time, eliminate yourselves, in the name of Jesus (Psalm 7:14-15; Psalm 57:6-7)
10. Poison prepared for me to step on or ingest for paralysis, I neutralize and render you null and void by the blood of Jesus, in the name of Jesus (Revelations 12:11)
11. The Bible says 'I will drink poison and it will not harm me', therefore I convert the food and drink I consume to the blood of Jesus and fire of the Holy Ghost, in the name of Jesus (Mark 16:17-18; Hebrews 12:24; Deuteronomy 4:24)
12. Every enchantment and bewitchment programmed into the beds I will sleep on and the chairs I will seat in, I command you to fail, in Jesus name (Numbers 23:23)

13. Any battle I am currently fighting because of my marriage/ relationship(s), I abort you by the power of the Holy Spirit, in the name of Jesus (Isaiah 10:27; Nahum 1:13)

14. Jesus, Man of War, go ahead of me and scatter every ungodly gathering and any plans against my destiny, in the name of Jesus (Exodus 15:3-10)

15. Every satanic ambush planned to displace me in my place of work/ business, be exposed and disgraced, in the name of Jesus (2 Corinthians 11:32-33)

16. All hidden hostile and hateful friends operating in my life, enter into error and expose yourselves, in the name of Jesus (Psalm 41:9-11)

17. I cover myself and my family with the blood of Jesus and envelope our lives with the fire of the Holy Ghost, in the name of Jesus (Revelations 12:11; Hebrews 12:29)

18. Father, I thank You for answered prayers, in Jesus name (Psalm 150:1-6; Psalm 20:1-9)

Crushing The Power Of Enchantment & Bewitchment

Scripture Reading: Deuteronomy 18:10-14; Leviticus 19:31; Leviticus 20:27, Revelations 21:8

Memory verse/Confession: Exodus 22:18 (KJV)

"Thou shalt not suffer a witch to live."

Explanation:

The strength of these prayers is in the understanding of what they entail. Enchantment manipulates and twists the destiny of an individual. Therefore, it is our prayer that with the knowledge of the Word of God and the fellowship of His Spirit, every one reading and praying these prayers will know that their freedom is already guaranteed because of the Blood. God's love and mercy surpasses anything, and so there is no power that is permitted to twist or manipulate any child of God.

THEME: WITCHCRAFT MUST DIE

1. I locate and crush every witchcraft plantation in my foundation, in the name of Jesus (Matthew 15:13)
2. Axe of the Holy Ghost, identify and cut down every tree of bewitchment growing in the garden of my life, in Jesus name (Matthew 3:10)
3. Witchcraft altars standing against my advancement, I dismantle and pull you down, in the name of Jesus (Judges 6:25-27)
4. Every voice of manipulation, speaking into my future, I silence you by the blood of Jesus, in the name of Jesus (Isaiah 54:17; Revelation 12:11)

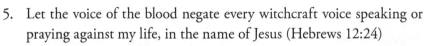
5. Let the voice of the blood negate every witchcraft voice speaking or praying against my life, in the name of Jesus (Hebrews 12:24)

6. Witchcraft gatherings against my destiny, scatter and disintegrate, in Jesus name (Isaiah 54:15)

7. Arrows of bewitchment fired against my relationship/marriage, I locate and roast you by fire, in Jesus name (Hebrews 12:29)

8. I decree there is no enchantment against me, neither divination against my household, in the name of Jesus (Numbers 23:23)

9. Anointing that cannot be bewitched, be released upon me, in the name of Jesus (Mark 16:17-18)

10. Holy Spirit, restore to me everything witchcraft agents and covens have stolen from me, in the name of Jesus (Joel 2:25-27)

11. Every witchcraft embargo assigned against my business, finances, friendships, marriage and ministry, break and release me by fire, in the name of Jesus (Isaiah 10:27; Nahum 1:13)

12. I destroy the foundation of witchcraft in my life and family, in the name of Jesus (Psalm 11:3; Matthew 15:13)

13. Every witchcraft poison programmed into my life through dreams, I neutralize and vomit it now, in the name of Jesus (Psalm 18:44-45)

14. I indentify and crush witchcraft agents feeding or defiling me sexually in my dreams, in the name of Jesus (Matthew 13:25; Revelations 13:10)

Addressing Dream & Other Related Attacks

<u>Scripture Reading:</u> Deuteronomy 29:29; Daniel 2:22; Psalm 25:14; Jeremiah 33:3, Psalm 91:1-16; Matthew 13:25

<u>Memory Verse/Confession</u>: Psalm 25:14

> *"The secret of the Lord is with them that fear him; and he will show them his covenant."*

<u>Explanation:</u>

It's been said that the dream world is a gateway to life or the physical realm. The truth is God communicates to us through dreams and the devil tends to also harass and initiate attacks against us through dreams. So it's important you are able to remember your dreams; but it's even more important to be able to properly regulate and control the outcome of your dreams through prayer.

THEME: PARALYZING DEMONIC STABILIZERS

1. Father Lord, I thank you for my life, in Jesus name (Psalm 103:1-5)
2. Holy Spirit, reveal to me the secret behind my life, in Jesus name (Psalm 25:14)
3. Lord, show me clearly who I am spiritually, in the name of Jesus (Deuteronomy 29:29)
4. Father Lord, reveal to me the secret behind my problem(s), in Jesus name (Jeremiah 3:33)

5. Lord Jesus, expose and show me in clear terms, the deep and dark covenants and agreements affecting my life negatively, in Jesus name (Daniel 2:22)

6. Holy Spirit, take me into my subconscious and expose by revelation the root of my problems, in the name of Jesus (Jeremiah 1:11-12)

7. You my spiritual eyes open by fire, so I can effectively remember all my dreams, in the name of Jesus (Deuteronomy 29:29; Psalm 25:14)

8. Any recurring dream being used to negatively manipulate my success, I neutralize and break your circle now, in the name of Jesus (Exodus 14:13-14; Nahum 1:13)

9. I cleanse myself by the blood of Jesus from spiritual leprosy within my foundation, in Jesus name (Hebrews 9:22; Revelations 12:11)

10. Every power attacking and polluting my dream life, receive divine disgrace, in Jesus name (Zechariah 3:1-5)

11. Every witchcraft activity targeted against my dream life, fail and backfire completely, in Jesus name (Revelations 13:10)

12. Eaters of flesh and drinkers of flesh, attacking me in the dream world, eat your own flesh and drink your own blood, in Jesus name (Isaiah 49:26)

13. Witchcraft caterers feeding me in my dreams, receive the judgment of fire and be roasted instantly, in the name of Jesus (Numbers 23:23; Hebrews 12:29)

14. Night and early morning caterers assigned to feed me in my dreams, eat your evil food and expire, in the name of Jesus (Psalm 53:4-5)

15. Any unprofitable dream that people have had concerning me, fail completely, in the name of Jesus (Isaiah 54:17)

16. Every foul spirit assigned to harass and terrorize me in my dreams, be arrested and terrorized by fire, in the name of Jesus (Deuteronomy 4:24)

17. Lord, deliver me from every ungodly recurring dream, in the name of Jesus (Psalm 59:1-5)

18. Every power coming to defile me sexually in my dreams, be roasted by fire, in Jesus name (Psalm 35:1-9)

19. I receive complete deliverance from every satanic haircut received in my dreams, in Jesus name (Obadiah 1:17; Judges 16:18-22)

20. I pull down evil altars in my mother and fathers house sponsoring satanic dreams and manifestations in my life, in the name of Jesus (Judges 6:11-16, 25-27)

21. Every marriage contracted with any spiritual entity causing me to constantly have sexual dreams, be annulled, in Jesus name (Isaiah 10:27; Colossians 2:14)

22. Every foundational blood covenant entered into on my behalf which the enemy is using to attack my dream life, break and release me by the blood of Jesus, in Jesus name (Revelations 12:11)

23. I scatter by thunder, any witchcraft gathering or deliberations which I continually dream about, in the name of Jesus (Psalm 144:1-6)

24. I revoke by the blood of Jesus, every foundational deficit anointing that has become a doorway for attack against me in my dreams and life, in Jesus name (Hebrews 9:22; Hebrews 12:24)

25. I cancel by the blood of Jesus, every misuse of my umbilical cord and placenta affecting my life negatively, in Jesus name (Revelations 12:11)

26. Father Lord, break and release me from all generational curses and covenants, working against my life, in Jesus name (Galatians 3:13)

27. Let all ungodly initiations and dedications done against me that have become a foundation for bad dreams and attacks against my destiny, be revoked by the blood of Jesus, in Jesus name (Colossians 2:14)

28. Any satanic incisions or marks working against my progress, be erased and blotted out by the blood of Jesus (Revelations 12:11)

29. Evil witch doctor enchanting against me in real life and my dreams, perish with your enchantments, in Jesus name (Numbers 23:23; Exodus 22:18-KJV)

30. Sacrifices offered against me at crossroads, which night and early morning caterers are using to feed me in my dreams, backfire to your senders, in Jesus name (Isaiah 49:26)

31. Spirit of poverty that is being projected against me by rats in my dreams, fail and backfire now, in Jesus name (Proverbs 11:8)

32. Any of my money and personal effects placed on evil altars to bewitch me, reject bewitchment by fire, in the name of Jesus (Hebrews 12:29)

33. Any evil covenants established and glory lost in former demonic offices, schools or homes I have lived in, I receive deliverance and

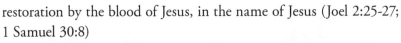

restoration by the blood of Jesus, in the name of Jesus (Joel 2:25-27; 1 Samuel 30:8)

34. Every conscious or unconscious covenant with dead relatives, friends or foes, release my destiny by fire, in Jesus name (Hebrews 12:29)

35. I receive deliverance from the operation of the spirit of death and hell manifesting through seeing burials, coffins and dead people in my dreams, in the name of Jesus (Psalm 118:17; Psalm 91:16; Job 5:19-27)

36. Every familiar spirit monitoring me in my dreams and life, be exposed and disgraced, in Jesus name (Deuteronomy 29:29; Isaiah 54:19)

37. I cancel by fire and the blood of Jesus, all witchcraft marks, scratches and labels I have received in dreams, in Jesus name (psalm 129:3)

38. Serpentine covenants and powers projecting snakes and creeping things against me in my dreams, be roasted by fire, in the name of Jesus (Isaiah 27:1; Hebrews 12:29)

39. Any satanic personality calling my name before ungodly altars, receive the slap of fire and the angels, in Jesus name (Lamentations 3:37)

40. Witchcraft powers attacking me through dogs in my dreams, receive divine disgrace, in the name of Jesus (Isaiah 59:19; Exodus 22:18 KJV)

41. Anyone offering demonic sacrifices against me, receive paralysis, in the name of Jesus (2 Thessalonians 1:6)

42. Marine witchcraft covenants and powers attacking me through swimming in rivers, seas, oceans and water related dreams, release my destiny by fire, in the name of Jesus (Obadiah 1:17; Deuteronomy 4:24)

43. Any dream criminal or strongman that will not let me go, die the death of Goliath now, in the name of Jesus (Matthew 13:25; 1 Samuel 17:48-51)

44. Every agreement entered into with the earth or waters against me, fail by fire, in Jesus name (Isaiah 7:5-7)

45. I thank the Lord for answered prayers, in Jesus name (Psalm 20:1-8)

46. I plead the blood of Jesus over my body, soul, spirit, family and business, in the name of Jesus (Revelations 12:11; Hebrews 12:24)

Miracle Healing Confessions & Prayers

These prayers comprise a catalogue of confessions which bring healing, ease and rest to the sick. With patience and faith in the Word of God, a hurting body, heart or soul will find the necessary solace and rest with these prayers. It is my prayer that lives will be changed and destinies reaffirmed to the glory of God. (Each confession is backed by Scriptural verses to confirm the authority of the confession).

Facts About Infirmity & God's Healing Provision

1. God wants you to be well and healthy
   - 1 John 1:2

2. Sickness has a spiritual root or source
   - Luke 13:11
   - Infirmity is as spiritual as it is physical because the physical has its source in the spiritual
   - Hebrews 11:3
   - 2 Corinthians 4:18
   - Romans 1:20

3. There is Satan or Demon Inspired Sickness
   - Matthew 9:32-33
   - Luke 13:13-16

4. Sickness can emanate from Natural Causes
   - John 9:1-6

5. Healing can be Gradual or Instant
   - Mark 8:22-26

6. Open Doors For Infirmity:
   A. Sin
   - John 5:14

   B. Lack of Proper Exercise of the Body
   - 1 Timothy 4:8-9

- 1 Corinthians 9:27 (ESV)
C. Wrong Diet, Gluttony and Carelessness
- 1 Corinthians 3:16-17
- Genesis 1:29-30
- Genesis 9:3
- Deuteronomy 14:8
- 1 Corinthians 6:12
- Proverbs 23:2
- Leviticus 3:17
- Leviticus 7:23-24
- Leviticus 3:12-13
- Acts 10:12-16
D. Pray and commit your food and bodies to God always
- 1 Corinthians 10:31
- Romans 12:1
- Exodus 23:25-26

7. Christ took our infirmities and bore our sicknesses
   - Matthew 8:16-17
   - 1 Peter 2:24

8. We have been healed by the stripes of Jesus Christ
   - Isaiah 53:4-5
   - 1 Peter 2:24

9. Praying and Confessing God's Word based on faith is necessary to actualize and take advantage of our healing heritage
   - Psalm 107:20
   - John 1:1-5, 14
   - Matthew 4:4
   - Hebrews 11:6
   - Hebrews 4:2
   - Matthew 6:25-26

10. Learn To Praise God in the midst of the storm
    - Habakkuk 3:17-19

- 1 Thessalonians 5:18
- Philippians 4:6-7
- You can praise yourself out of the storm
- Praising God in the midst of the storm is an indication you trust and rely on Him for intervention and deliverance

11. You can Pray yourself out of the storm
   - James 5:13-18
   - Psalm 118:5-7
   - 1 Thessalonians 5:17
   - Psalm 50:15

12. You can also wear the enemy out by your faith, persistence and refusal to quit or give up
   - Job 13:15
   - 1 John 5:4, 13-15
   - Hebrews 11:2

Miracle Healing Confessions

1. God's Word has saved my life.

Scripture Confession: Proverbs 4:20-22

> *"My son, give attention to my words; Incline your ear to my sayings. Do not let them depart from your eyes; Keep them in the midst of your heart. For they are life to those who find them, and health to all their flesh."*

2. God's Word can never ever fail.

Scripture Confession: Joshua 21:45

> *"Not a word failed of any good thing which the LORD had spoken to the house of Israel. All came to pass."*

3. In all situations bless the Lord!

Scripture Confession: Psalm 103:1-5

> *"Bless the LORD, O my soul; and all that is within me, bless His holy name! Bless the LORD, O my soul, and forget not all His benefits: Who forgives all your iniquities, Who heals all your diseases, Who redeems your life from destruction, Who crowns you with lovingkindness and tender mercies, Who satisfies your mouth with good things, So that your youth is renewed like the eagles."*

4. The Lord's Spirit of Life has made my body alive.

Scripture Confession: Romans 8:11

> *"But if the Spirit of Him who raised Jesus from the dead dwells in you, He who raised Christ from the dead will also give life to your mortal bodies through His Spirit who dwells in you."*

5. God will have mercy on me and heal me.

Scripture Confession: Psalm 6:2

> *"Have mercy on me, O LORD, for I am weak; O LORD, heal me, for my bones are troubled."*

6. It is God's will for me to be healed.

Scripture Confession: Psalm 30:2

> *"O LORD my God, I cried out to You, And You healed me."*

7. When I do what God says, I will be healed.

Scripture Confession: Exodus 15:26

> *"If you* **(I)** *diligently heed the voice of the LORD your* **(my)** *God and do what is right in His sight, give ear to His commandments and keep all His statutes, I* **(He)** *will put none of the diseases on you* **(me)** *which I* **(He)** *have brought on the Egyptians. For I am* **(He is)** *the LORD who heals you* **(me)."***

8. Seek the Lord and healing is mine.

Scripture Confession: 2 Chronicles 7:14

> *"If My people who are called by My name will humble themselves, and pray and seek My face, and turn from their wicked ways, then I will hear from heaven, and will forgive their sin and heal their land."*

9. God has taken every sickness away from me.

Scripture Confession: Deuteronomy 7:15

> *"And the LORD will take away from you all sickness, and will afflict you with none of the terrible diseases of Egypt which you have known, but will lay them on all those who hate you."*

10. God's Word has healed me.

Scripture Confession: Psalm 107:20

> *"He sent His word and healed them, and delivered them from their destructions."*

11. God's Word gives me life!

Scripture Confession: Psalm 118:17

> *"I shall not die, but live, and declare the works of the LORD."*

12. I choose life!

(i) Scripture Confession: Deuteronomy 30:19

> *"I call heaven and earth as witnesses today against you, that I have set before you life and death, blessing and cursing; therefore choose life, that both you and your descendants may live."*

(ii) Scripture Confession: Psalm 91:16

> *"With long life I will satisfy him, and show him My salvation."*

13. I am already healed!

(i) Scripture Confession: Isaiah 53:5

> *"He was wounded for our transgressions, He was bruised for our iniquities; the chastisement for our peace was upon Him, and by His stripes we are healed."*

(ii) Scripture Confession: *Jeremiah 30:17*

> *"For I will restore health to you and heal you of your wounds,' says the LORD, 'because they called you an outcast saying: "This is Zion; No one seeks her."*

14. I have power and authority over my health.

Scripture Confession: Matthew 18:18

> *"Assuredly, I say to you, whatever you bind on earth will be bound in heaven, and whatever you loose on earth will be loosed in heaven."*

15. I agree with my faith partners that I am healed, so I am healed.
 Scripture Confession: Matthew 18:19

> *"Again I say to you that if two of you agree on earth concerning anything that they ask, it will be done for them by My Father in heaven.*

16. I say I am healed so I am healed.

Scripture Confession: Mark 11:22-23

> *"So Jesus answered and said to them, "Have faith in God. For assuredly, I say to you, whoever says to this mountain, Be removed and be cast into the sea, and does not doubt in his heart, but believes that those things he says will be done, he will have whatever he says."*

17. I have faith to be healed.

Scripture Confession: Mark 11:24

> *"Therefore I say to you, whatever things you ask when you pray, believe that you receive them, and you will have them.*

18. I state my case to you God; I claim healing.

Scripture Confession: Isaiah 43:25-26

> *"Even I, am He who blots out your transgressions for my own sake; And I will not remember your sins. Put me in remembrance; Let us contend together; State your case, that you may be acquitted."*

19. As I lay my hands on myself I say I am healed in Jesus Name.

(i) Scripture Confession: Mark 16:17-18

> *"And these signs will follow those who believe: In My name they will cast out demons; they will speak with new tongues; "they will take up serpents; and if they drink anything deadly, it will by no means hurt them; they will lay hands on the sick, and they will recover."*

(ii) Scripture Confession: Jeremiah 17:14

> *"Heal me, O LORD, and I shall be healed; Save me, and I shall be saved, For You are my praise."*

20. Lord, renew Your covenant of life and sustenance over me, in Jesus Name.

(i) Scripture Confession: John 10:10

> *"The thief does not come except to steal, and to kill, and to destroy. I have come that they may have life, and that they may have it more abundantly."*

(ii) Scripture Confession: Hebrews 10:23

> *"Let us hold fast the confession of our hope without wavering, for He who promised is faithful."*

21. I must be confident in the Lord of lords.

(i) Scripture Confession: Hebrews 10:35

> *"Therefore do not cast away your confidence, which has great reward."*

(ii) Scripture Confession: Joel 3:10

> *"Beat your plowshares into swords and your pruning hooks
> into spears; Let the weak say, 'I am strong.'"*

22. God wants for me to be well and to prosper.

Scripture Confession: 3 John 1:2 (KJV)

> *"Beloved, I wish above all things that thou mayest prosper
> and be in health, even as thy soul prospereth."*

23. God wants to heal and raise me up in time of sickness.

Scripture Confession: James 5:14-15

> *"Is anyone among you sick? Let him call for the elders of the
> church, and let them pray over him, anointing him with oil
> in the name of the Lord. And the prayer of faith will save the
> sick, and the Lord will raise him up. And if he has committed
> sins, he will be forgiven."*

24. Jesus paid the price for my healing when He died on the cross for me.

Scripture Confession: 1 Peter 2:24

> *"Who Himself bore our sins in His own body on the tree, that
> we, having died to sins, might live for righteousness; by whose
> stripes you were healed."*

25. God wants me to come confidently to His Throne of Grace, and receive healing, for it is His Will.

Scripture Confession: 1 John 5:14-15

> *"Now this is the confidence that we have in Him, that if we ask anything according to His will, He hears us. And if we know that He hears us, whatever we ask, we know that we have the petitions that we have asked of Him."*

Scripture Confession: 1 John 3:21-22

> *"Beloved, if our heart does not condemn us, we have confidence toward God. And whatever we ask we receive from Him, because we keep His commandments and do those things that are pleasing in His sight."*

26. I rebuke anything in me that is not from God!

Scripture Confession: 2 Timothy 1:7

> *"For God has not given us a spirit of fear, but of power and of love and of a sound mind."*

27. I cast down those thoughts and imaginations that don't line up with the Word of God for my life.

Scripture Confession: 2 Corinthians 10:4-5

> *"For the weapons of our warfare are not carnal but mighty in God for pulling down strongholds, casting down arguments and every high thing that exalts itself against the knowledge of God, bringing every thought into captivity to the obedience of Christ."*

28. I fight the good fight of faith as it relates to my healing, and take my healing by force, in Jesus Name.

    Scripture Confession: Ephesians 6:10-17

    "Finally, my brethren, be strong in the Lord and in the power of His might. Put on the whole armor of God that you may be able to stand against the wiles of the devil. For we do not wrestle against flesh and blood, but against principalities, against powers, against the rulers of the darkness of this age, and against spiritual hosts of wickedness in the heavenly places. Therefore take up the whole armor of God that you may be able to withstand in the evil day, and having done all, to stand. Stand therefore, having girded your waist with truth, having put on the breastplate of righteousness, and having shod your feet with the preparation of the gospel of peace; above all, taking the shield of faith with which you will be able to quench all the fiery darts of the wicked one. And take the helmet of salvation, and the sword of the Spirit, which is the word of God."

29. I will give testimonies about the work You have done in my life oh Lord, to the glory of Your name!
    Scripture Confession: Revelations 12:11

    "And they overcame him by the blood of the Lamb and by the word of their testimony, and they did not love their lives to the death."

30. I am free in the LORD, because He has set me free, and very free indeed!

Scripture Confession: Nahum 1:9

    "What do you conspire against the LORD? He will make an utter end of it. Affliction will not rise up a second time."

31. As I receive from the Lord, I know He will and has restored me.

(i) Scripture Confession: Hosea 6:1

> *"Come, and let us return to the LORD; For He has torn, but He will heal us; He has stricken, but He will bind us up."*

(ii) Scripture Confession: Isaiah 54:17

> *"No weapon formed against you shall prosper, and every tongue which rises against you in judgment you shall condemn. This is the heritage of the servants of the LORD, and their righteousness is from me," says the LORD."*

(iii) Scripture Confession: Isaiah 41:10

> *"Fear not, for I am with you; be not dismayed, for I am your God. I will strengthen you, Yes, I will help you, I will uphold you with My righteous right hand."*

(iv) Scripture Confession: 1 John 5:4

> *"For whatever is born of God overcomes the world. And this is the victory that has overcome the world—our faith."*

Yoke Breaking & Other Healing Scripture Confession Prayers

1. Personal, parental and ancestral curses fighting against me, break right now!

   (i) Scripture Confession: Galatians 3:13

   > *"Christ has redeemed us from the curse of the law, having become a curse for us (for it is written, "Cursed is everyone who hangs on a tree"*

2. Records of foundational, ancestral and personal wrongdoing the enemy is using against me, be blotted out by the blood of Jesus.

   (i) Scripture Confession: Colossians 2:14-15

   > *"Having wiped out the handwriting of requirements that was against us, which was contrary to us. And He has taken it out of the way, having nailed it to the cross. 15 Having disarmed principalities and powers, He made a public spectacle of them, triumphing over them in it."*

3. I receive the help of God to crush every persistent and unrepentant enemy.

   (i) Scripture Confession: Psalm 18:29-42

   > *"For by You I can run through a troop, by my God I can leap over a wall. As for God, His way is perfect; the word of the*

Lord is proven; He is a shield to all who trust in Him. For who is God, except the Lord? And who is a rock, except our God? It is God who arms me with strength, and makes my way perfect. He makes my feet like the feet of deer, and sets me on my high places. He teaches my hands to make war, so that my arms can bend a bow of bronze. You have also given me the shield of Your salvation; Your right hand has held me up, Your gentleness has made me great. You enlarged my path under me, so my feet did not slip. I have pursued my enemies and overtaken them; neither did I turn back again till they were destroyed. I have wounded them, so that they could not rise; they have fallen under my feet. For You have armed me with strength for the battle; You have subdued under me those who rose up against me. You have also given me the necks of my enemies, so that I destroyed those who hated me. They cried out, but there was none to save; even to the Lord, but He did not answer them. Then I beat them as fine as the dust before the wind; I cast them out like dirt in the streets."

(ii) Scripture Confession: Psalm 18:44-45

"As soon as they hear of me they obey me; the foreigners submit to me. The foreigners fade away, and come frightened from their hideouts."

4. The Lord is my strength, my protector and the lifter up of my head.

(i) Scripture Confession: Psalm 27:1-6

"The Lord is my light and my salvation; whom shall I fear? The Lord is the strength of my life; of whom shall I be afraid? When the wicked came against me to eat up my flesh, my enemies and foes, they stumbled and fell. Though an army may encamp against me, my heart shall not fear; though war may rise against me, in this I will be confident. One thing I have desired of the Lord, that will I seek: that I may dwell

in the house of the Lord all the days of my life, to behold the beauty of the Lord, and to inquire in His temple. For in the time of trouble He shall hide me in His pavilion; in the secret place of His tabernacle He shall hide me; He shall set me high upon a rock. And now my head shall be lifted up above my enemies all around me; therefore I will offer sacrifices of joy in His tabernacle; I will sing, yes, I will sing praises to the Lord."

5. Father, You are the fighter of my battles, defend me in every battle I presently face.

    (i) Scripture Confession: Psalm 35:1-9

    "Plead my cause, O Lord, with those who strive with me; fight against those who fight against me. Take hold of shield and buckler, and stand up for my help. Also draw out the spear, and stop those who pursue me. Say to my soul, "I am your salvation." Let those be put to shame and brought to dishonor who seek after my life; Let those be turned back and brought to confusion who plot my hurt. Let them be like chaff before the wind,

    And let the angel of the Lord chase them. Let their way be dark and slippery, and let the angel of the Lord pursue them. For without cause they have hidden their net for me in a pit, which they have dug without cause for my life. Let destruction come upon him unexpectedly, and let his net that he has hidden catch himself; into that very destruction let him fall. And my soul shall be joyful in the Lord; It shall rejoice in His salvation."

6. The Lord is my refuge and strength; I refuse to fear.

    (i) Scripture Confession: Psalm 46:1-3

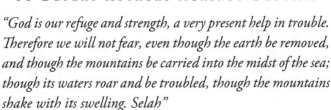

"God is our refuge and strength, a very present help in trouble. Therefore we will not fear, even though the earth be removed, and though the mountains be carried into the midst of the sea; though its waters roar and be troubled, though the mountains shake with its swelling. Selah"

(ii) Scripture Confession: Psalm 46:10-11

"Be still, and know that I am God; I will be exalted among the nations, I will be exalted in the earth! The Lord of hosts is with us; the God of Jacob is our refuge. Selah"

7. God of deliverance, defend me against those who rise up against me.

(i) Scripture Confession: Psalm 59:1-2

"Deliver me from my enemies, O my God; defend me from those who rise up against me. Deliver me from the workers of iniquity, and save me from bloodthirsty men."

8. I receive provision for my vision as I passionately pursue God's purpose for my life.

(i) Scripture Confession: Psalm 68:19

"Blessed be the Lord, who daily loads us with benefits, the God of our salvation! Selah"

9. As I dwell in the secret place of the Most High, I abide under the shadow of the almighty!

(i) Scripture Confession: Psalm 91:1-13

"He who dwells in the secret place of the Most High shall abide under the shadow of the Almighty. I will say of the Lord, "He is my refuge and my fortress; my God, in Him I

will trust." Surely He shall deliver you from the snare of the fowler and from the perilous pestilence. He shall cover you with His feathers, and under His wings you shall take refuge; His truth shall be your shield and buckler. You shall not be afraid of the terror by night, nor of the arrow that flies by day, nor of the pestilence that walks in darkness, nor of the destruction that lays waste at noonday. A thousand may fall at your side, and ten thousand at your right hand; but it shall not come near you. Only with your eyes shall you look, and see the reward of the wicked. Because you have made the Lord, who is my refuge, even the Most High, your dwelling place, no evil shall befall you, nor shall any plague come near your dwelling; for He shall give His angels charge over you, to keep you in all your ways. In their hands they shall bear you up, lest you dash your foot against a stone. You shall tread upon the lion and the cobra, the young lion and the serpent you shall trample underfoot."

10. I receive grace to expand and occupy till Christ comes.

    (i) Scripture Confession: Isaiah 54:3-4

    "For you shall expand to the right and to the left, and your descendants will inherit the nations, and make the desolate cities inhabited. "Do not fear, for you will not be ashamed; neither be disgraced, for you will not be put to shame; for you will forget the shame of your youth, and will not remember the reproach of your widowhood anymore."

11. God is with me; therefore I cannot be bewitched, ambushed or defeated.

    (i) Scripture Confession: Isaiah 54:17

    "No weapon formed against you shall prosper, and every tongue which rises against you in judgment you shall

condemn. This is the heritage of the servants of the Lord,
and their righteousness is from Me," says the Lord."

12. I claim and receive double honor in place of my shame, in the precious
name of Jesus.

Scripture Confession: Isaiah 61:7

"Instead of your shame you shall have double honor, and
instead of confusion they shall rejoice in their portion.
Therefore in their land they shall possess double; everlasting
joy shall be theirs."

Deliverance From Liver & Stomach Sicknesses

Scripture Reading: 2 Chronicles 21:12-19; Psalm 1:1-6; Psalm 20:1-2; Psalm 30:2

Memory Verse/Confession: 2 Chronicles 21:18

> *"After all this the LORD struck him in his intestines with an incurable disease."*

Explanation:

Liver disease can be very deadly, but there is healing in the name and stripes of Jesus. These are unique prayers to help us pray ourselves out of terminal illness. Please pray them aggressively and with faith.

THEME: LORD, ARISE WITH HEALING IN YOUR WINGS

1. Father Lord, let Your sent Word begin to heal my jaundiced eyes now, in the name of Jesus (Psalm 107:19-21)
2. Father Lord, deliver me from abdominal pain and swelling caused by liver disease, in the name of Jesus (Obadiah 1:17)
3. Every power of infirmity affecting my lungs, liver and kidney, release my life by fire and by force, in the name of Jesus (Exodus 15:26)
4. I receive divine relief from itchiness of the skin and dark colored urine associated with liver problems, in the name of Jesus (Exodus 23:25)
5. Holy Ghost fire, locate and burn to ashes all lumps, tumors, and evil growths, hiding in any part of my body, in the name of Jesus (Psalm 30:2)

6. I receive miraculous healing from every yoke of terminal illness by the stripes of our Lord Jesus Christ, in the name of Jesus (Proverbs 4:20-22)

7. Every arrow of sickness fired into my body to cause chronic fatigue and pale, bloody or tar colored stool, come out by fire and return to sender, in the name of Jesus (Revelation 13:10)

8. I claim healing, wholeness, and divine health from nausea, vomiting and loss of appetite connected to liver and stomach diseases, in the name of Jesus (Job 22:28 - KJV)

9. Every tendency to bruise easily as a result of liver complications be healed instantly, in the name of Jesus (Matthew 8:16-17)

10. Whatever is causing my liver to shut down, I shut you down completely, in the name of Jesus[1] (Proverbs 11:8)

Healing From All Forms of Cancer

Scripture Reading: Matthew 19:21; Luke 1:37; Psalm 20:1-8; Acts 3:1-16

Memory Verse/Confession: Exodus 15:26

> *"And said, "If you diligently heed the voice of the LORD your God and do what is right in His sight, give ear to His commandments and keep all His statutes, I will put none of the diseases on you which I have brought on the Egyptians. For I am the LORD who heals you."*

Explanation:

Cancer is a slow killer and a very deadly disease. But I have heard it said that if God can move mountains, God can move cancer. These prayers are anointed to arrest and destroy the seed and symptoms of cancer.

THEME: HEALING IS MY HERITAGE

1. I agree with God's Word that by His stripes, I am healed of unexplained weight loss and fever as a result of cancer, in the name of Jesus (Isaiah 53:4-5)
2. Healing is my bread, and as I snack on the Bread of life, I am healed of pain and skin changes relating to cancer, in the name of Jesus (Matthew 15:21-28)
3. I uproot every evil cancerous growth or tumor in any part of my body, in the name of Jesus (Matthew 15:13)

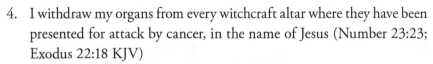

4. I withdraw my organs from every witchcraft altar where they have been presented for attack by cancer, in the name of Jesus (Number 23:23; Exodus 22:18 KJV)

5. Let every demonic yoke of cancer manifesting as change in bowel habits, bladder function, and sores that do not heal, be destroyed, in the name of Jesus (Psalm 103:2-4)

6. I drink the blood and eat the flesh of the Lord Jesus Christ for healing from cancer, and restoration and strength, in the name of Jesus (Revelations 12:11; Psalm 41:2-3)

7. Cancer that is attacking my family members sponsored by foundational covenants, break and release me by fire, in Jesus Name (Galatians 3:13; Isaiah 10:27)

8. I receive deliverance from every dream attack through which cancer is being planted in my life, in the name of Jesus (Matthew 8:5-17)

9. I decree that I am who and what God's Word says I am; therefore I reject white patches inside the mouth or white spots on the tongue as a result of cancer, in the name of Jesus (Psalm 147:3; Jeremiah 17:14)

10. Unusual bleeding or discharge as a result of cancer or terminal illness, release my destiny now, in the name of Jesus (Matthew 9:35; Luke 8:43-48)

11. I rebuke and bind every thickening or lump in the breast or other parts of the body that are symptoms of the attack of cancer, in the name of Jesus (Matthew 16:19; Luke 8:49-56)

12. Cancerous symptoms manifesting as indigestion or trouble swallowing and recent skin changes, be extinguished by the blood of Jesus, in the name of Jesus (Revelations 12:11; Revelations 21:4; James 5:16)

13. I receive healing and deliverance from all cough and hoarseness in my voice resulting from cancer that refuses to go away, in the name of Jesus (1 Peter 2:24)[2]

Attacking The Root of High Blood Pressure & Heart Disease(s)

<u>Scripture Reading</u>: Isaiah 41:10; Jeremiah 33:6; 1 Peter 2:24; James 5:14-15

<u>Memory Verse/Confession</u>: 1 Samuel 25:36-37 (MSG)

> *"When Abigail got home she found Nabal presiding over a huge banquet. He was in high spirits—and very, very drunk. So she didn't tell him anything of what she'd done until morning. But in the morning, after Nabal had sobered up, she told him the whole story. Right then and there he had a heart attack and fell into a coma. About ten days later God finished him off and he died."*

<u>Explanation</u>:

Heart disease manifesting as hypertension or high blood pressure can be very deadly as it can kill in an instant, since it gives no warning whatsoever. Below are prayers to help combat the problems associated with this disease.

THEME: THE BREAD OF THE CHILDREN

1. Every symptom and consequence of high blood pressure with symptoms of chest pain, nausea, sweating, shortness of breath, and dizziness, be exposed and disgraced, in the name of Jesus (Isaiah 10:27; Nahum 1:13; Matthew 8:17-18)

2. Stubborn illnesses in my life manifesting as chest pain which may radiate or travel to the arms, back, neck, or jaw, be destroyed by the

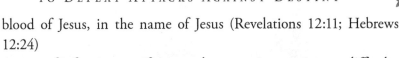

blood of Jesus, in the name of Jesus (Revelations 12:11; Hebrews 12:24)

3. Arrows of infirmity manifesting as hypertension causing me difficulty in sleeping, go back to your sender, in the name of Jesus (Proverbs 11:8)

4. Every tree of terminal illness growing in the field of my life causing me to urinate unnecessarily at night, wither from your roots, in the name of Jesus (Matthew 15:13; Luke 3:9)

5. I drink the blood of Jesus and eat the fire of the Holy Ghost, in Jesus name (Jeremiah 17:14)

6. Healing virtue in the stripes of Jesus flow from the crown of my head to the sole of my feet and decongest my heart of every congestion in my arteries, in the name of Jesus (Isaiah 53:4-5)

7. Every symptom and manifestation of high blood pressure, including constant headaches and fatigue, be neutralized completely by the fire of the Holy Ghost, in the name of Jesus (Hebrews 12:29)

8. Sun of righteousness, arise with healing in Your wings for my sake, and heal me of bloating and irregular pulse, in the name of Jesus (Malachi 4:2)

9. I curse and uproot by the roots every tree of hypertension, and high blood pressure, attacking my health, in the name of Jesus (Matthew 15:13)

10. O Lord, deliver me from shortness of breath and swelling of the feet and ankles, in the name of Jesus (Psalm 50:15)

11. Every discomfort in areas of my upper body as a result of hypertension, including pain in one or both arms, the back, neck, jaw or stomach, release me now, in the name of Jesus[3]

Destroying The Spirit and Physical Manifestation of AIDS & HIV

Scripture Reading: Exodus 12:13; Exodus 9:14-16; Matthew 8:16-17; Leviticus 26:16

Memory Verse/Confession: Leviticus 26:21

> *"'Then, if you walk contrary to Me, and are not willing to obey Me, I will bring on you seven times more plagues, according to your sins."*

Explanation:

The HIV virus is a very deadly disease that ultimately leads to the pain, suffering and untimely death of those infected. This is why abstinence is the best principle when it comes to matters of sexual involvement before marriage. Also, as it concerns marriage the issue of fidelity must be taken seriously.

THEME: I AM HEALED BY HIS STRIPES

1. I root out by fire, every tree of HIV growing in the garden of my life, in the name of Jesus (Matthew 15:13)
2. Blood of Jesus, identify and terminate every legal ground the devil is using to afflict me with constant fever and profuse night sweats relating to the AIDS virus, in the name of Jesus (Isaiah 38:1-8)
3. I roast by fire every symptom of swollen glands associated with the HIV virus, in the name of Jesus (Hebrews 12:29)

4. Because I have been redeemed by the blood and now belong to the family of God, I release myself from every sore throat and body rash connected with AIDS, in the name of Jesus (1 Peter 2:24)

5. Every wicked handwriting of incurable disease written on any satanic blackboard against my health, be erased by the blood of Jesus, in the name of Jesus (Colossians 2:14)

6. I receive forgiveness and healing from sexual promiscuity and other mistakes I have made that have introduced HIV with symptoms of constant fatigue, extreme and unexplained tiredness and rapid weight loss into my life, in the name of Jesus (Psalm 50:15)

7. My Father and My God, heal me of every symptom of AIDS manifesting as muscle and joint aches and pains, because Christ has healed me by His stripes, in the name of Jesus (Isaiah 53:4-5)

8. Prolonged swelling of the lymph glands in the armpits, groin, or neck in my body associated with the HIV virus, be healed instantly, in the name of Jesus (Jeremiah 33:6)

9. Diarrhea that lasts for more than a week and sores of the mouth, anus, or genitals afflicting me due to the AIDS virus, release me completely now, in the name of Jesus (Psalm 103:2-4)

10. Repeated attacks of pneumonia, as well as red, brown, pink, or purplish blotches on or under the skin or inside the mouth, nose, or eyelids as a result of the acquired immune deficiency syndrome in my system, die and let me go, in the name of Jesus (James 5:14-16)

11. I receive deliverance from memory loss, depression, and other neurologic disorders and blurred and distorted vision flowing from the HIV virus, in the name of Jesus[4] (3 John 1:2; Matthew 10:8)

Prayers Against The Ebola Virus and Sickness

Scripture Reading: 2 Chronicles 7:13-14; Luke 21:11; Mark 5:26; Jeremiah 30:13; Psalm 18:6

Memory Verse/Confession: Deuteronomy 28:21-22

> *"The LORD will make the plague cling to you until He has consumed you from the land which you are going to possess. The LORD will strike you with consumption, with fever, with inflammation, with severe burning fever, with the sword, with scorching, and with mildew; they shall pursue you until you perish."*

Explanation:

The Ebola virus is one of the latest diseases ravaging humanity; especially in third world countries. We can prevent any sickness or disease from taking residence in our lives as long as we apply Gods Word in faith. These prayers have been carefully put together to help us arrest the menace of this virus.

THEME: HEAL ME LORD & I WILL BE HEALED

1. I command every diagnoses and symptom of Ebola causing me recurring fever to release me completely, in the name of Jesus (Obadiah 1:17)
2. Fire of God, locate and consume the roots of severe headaches resulting from Ebola growing in my body, in the name of Jesus (Hebrews 12:29)

3. Balm of Gilead, identify the hiding place of Ebola in my life that is causing me weakness and destruction, in Jesus name (Jeremiah 8:21-22)

4. I receive healing from Ebola related diarrhea by the stripes of Jesus, in the name of Jesus (1 Peter 2:24)

5. Let every deposit of Ebola in my life responsible for constant vomiting receive fire and be roasted, in the name of Jesus (Deuteronomy 4:24)

6. I command every arrow of Ebola presently operating in any department of my life as abdominal or stomach pain to be neutralized by the blood of Jesus, in the name of Jesus (Revelations 12:11)

7. Unexplained hemorrhage, bleeding and bruising in any part of my body, receive healing by the finger of God, in the name of Jesus (Luke 5:17)

8. I exempt and remove myself from possible infection by the Ebola virus circulating in my community, in the name of Jesus (2 Timothy 4:18)

9. Every doorway of sickness the enemy may want to use to access my life, I close you permanently, in the name of Jesus (Revelations 3:7)

10. Holy Spirit, grant me immunity from the Ebola Virus and other terminal diseases the enemy is using to waste lives, in the name of Jesus[5] (Psalm 138:6-8)

Relief From Fractures & Bone Related Diseases

Scripture Reading: Proverbs 17:22; Psalm 103:2-4; Psalm 23:25; 2 Chronicles 16:12-13

Memory Verse/Confession: Job 30:16-17

> *"And now my soul is poured out because of my plight; the days of affliction take hold of me. My bones are pierced in me at night, and my gnawing pains take no rest."*

Explanation:

When bones are fractured or broken it is difficult for the individual to function, because it the bones that carry the total structure of the body. These prayers are meant to combat the root, symptoms and effects of bone related complications.

THEME: HE BORE OUR INFIRMITIES

Prayer Song: I say yes, yes, Lord; I say yes, yes, Lord; I say yes Lord, I say yes Lord; I say yes, yes, Lord; I say yes, yes, Lord!

1. Isaiah 53:5B says I am healed by His stripes, therefore I claim complete healing from cancer in my bones manifesting as primary malignancy, in the name of Jesus
2. Psalm 107:20 says Christ sent His Word and has healed me, therefore I anchor my healing and deliverance from cancer that has spread to my

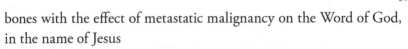
bones with the effect of metastatic malignancy on the Word of God, in the name of Jesus

3. Malachi 4:2 says 'The Sun of Righteousness has arisen with healing in His wings for me', and I therefore receive the fullness of God's healing from disruption of blood supply as in sickle cell anemia, in the name of Jesus

4. 1 John 3:8B says 'The Son of God was manifested to destroy the works of the devil', and I hereby stand on the authority of God's Word and destroy every attack of the devil relating to infected bones or osteomyelitis in my life, in the name of Jesus

5. Matthew 15:13 says, 'Every plant my heavenly Father has not planted will be uprooted', so I uproot every plantation of leukemia in any bones in my body, in the name of Jesus

6. Toddler fracture which is a type of stress fracture that occurs in toddlers, wither and expire now, in the name of Jesus (Matthew 3:10)

7. Matthew 8:17 says 'He took our infirmities and bore our sicknesses, and I hereby rebuke and expel every presence of bone infection in my body and life, in the name of Jesus

8. Luke 11:14 declares 'Christ cast out a mute spirit and the dumb man spoke', therefore I command every foul spirit sponsoring loss of mineralization or osteoporosis in my life to be bound and cast out, in the name of Jesus

9. It is written in Luke 10:19 that 'Christ has given us authority to trample on serpents and scorpions, and over all the power of the enemy', I therefore trample upon every serpent and scorpion of bone disease and fracture programmed against me, in the name of Jesus

10. Any overuse of my bones causing me bone disease or infection, be healed instantly, in the name of Jesus[6] (Matthew 8:16-17)

Power To Subdue & Overcome Insanity & Mental Illnesses

Scripture Reading: 2 Peter 2:15-16; 1 Samuel 21:12-15; 1 Samuel 19:20-24; 1 Samuel 16:14-23

Memory Verse/Confession: Daniel 4:33-34

> *"That very hour the word was fulfilled concerning Nebuchadnezzar; he was driven from men and ate grass like oxen; his body was wet with the dew of heaven till his hair had grown like eagles' feathers and his nails like birds' claws. And at the end of the time I, Nebuchadnezzar, lifted my eyes to heaven, and my understanding returned to me; and I blessed the Most High and praised and honored Him who lives forever: for His dominion is an everlasting dominion, and His kingdom is from generation to generation."*

Explanation:

When the mind is sick the entire man is sick. So the wholeness of the mind is central to the proper function of the entire human being. These prayers will help us understand and overcome mental illness.

THEME: HEALED BY HIS BROKEN BODY

1. I declare I am healed and receive my healing from insanity and mental illness instantly, in the name of Jesus (Acts 26:23)
2. Little foxes spoiling the vine of my mind and sanity, eat poison and die, in the name of Jesus (Songs of Solomon 2:15)

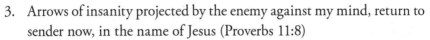
3. Arrows of insanity projected by the enemy against my mind, return to sender now, in the name of Jesus (Proverbs 11:8)

4. Every root of mental imbalance manifesting as confused thinking in my life, wither completely, in the name of Jesus (Matthew 15:13)

5. Sickness of the mind sponsoring prolonged depression, sadness or irritability in my life, be healed immediately, in the name of Jesus (Proverbs 4:23; Proverbs 23:7A)

6. Feelings of extreme highs and lows and excessive fears, worries and anxieties flowing from instability of the mind, release me completely, in the name of Jesus (Isaiah 10:27)

7. Symptoms of social withdrawal and dramatic changes in eating or sleeping habits, be neutralized by the blood of Jesus, in the name of Jesus (Revelations 12:11)

8. Strange thoughts or delusions and seeing or hearing things that aren't there or hallucinations that are the result of mental issues, be exterminated, in the name of Jesus (Jeremiah 33:6)

9. Stripes of our Lord Jesus Christ, establish healing in every department of my life concerning strong feelings of anger and frequent outbursts of anger, in the name of Jesus (Isaiah 53:4-5)

10. I confess and claim God's healing and wholeness in my mind, and reject persistent nightmares, excessive worry or anxiety and refusal to go to bed due to hyperactivity, in the name of Jesus (Job 22:28 – KJV; 1 Peter 2:24)

11. Growing inability to cope with daily problems and activities, as well as suicidal thoughts and defiance of authority resulting from unhealthy mental pressures, loose your hold over my life immediately, in the name of Jesus (2 Timothy 1:7)

12. I break the hold of substance abuse, numerous unexplained physical ailments, and prolonged negative mood, often accompanied by poor appetite connected with mental illness, in the name of Jesus[7] (Nahum 1:13)

Breaking Free From Sleeplessness & The Spirit of Insomnia

<u>Scripture Reading</u>: Daniel 2:1; Hebrews 4:1-16; Esther 6:1; Luke 22:39-46; Ecclesiastes 2:23

<u>Memory Verse/Confession</u>: Genesis 31:40

> *"There I was! In the day the drought consumed me, and the frost by night, and my sleep departed from my eyes."*

<u>Explanation</u>:

Insomnia is sleeplessness that may be the result of medical, psychological, physical or spiritual factors. The Lord gives His beloved rest and sleep according to Psalm 127:2, so the inability to sleep can be conquered. These prayers will help you overcome this condition.

THEME: THE BALM OF GILEAD

Prayer Song: You are the Lord that healeth me; You are the Lord my healer; You sent Your Word and healed my disease…

1. Balm of Gilead, release Your healing oil upon me for instant healing from difficulty falling asleep at night, in the name of Jesus (Jeremiah 8:21-22)
2. Sickness motivated by insomnia that causes me to awaken and stay wake during the night, I eliminate you by the blood of Jesus, in the name of Jesus (Job 30:16-17)

3. Deposits of sickness hiding in any department of my life causing irritability, depression or anxiety, melt by fire and be flushed out by the blood of Jesus, in the name of Jesus (Hebrews 12:29; Revelations 12:11)

4. Daytime tiredness or sleepiness causing me difficulty paying attention, focusing on tasks or remembering, release me now, in the name of Jesus (Psalm 107:20)

5. Awakening too early that makes me feel not well rested after a night's sleep, I command you to let me go, in the name of Jesus (Psalm 77:1-11)

6. Any sickness relating to sleeplessness, frustration and crankiness flowing in the genes of my family, I am not your candidate, in the name of Jesus (Colossians 2:14)

7. Generational illnesses working in my family bloodline causing daytime tiredness or sleepiness, you will no longer prosper in my life, in the name of Jesus (Galatians 3:13)

8. Distress in the stomach and intestines or gastrointestinal tract afflicting my life, die prematurely, in the name of Jesus (Job 5:12)

9. It is written that by His stripes I am healed, therefore I receive instant healing by the stripes of Jesus from tension headaches and ongoing worries that steal my sleep, in the name of Jesus (1 Peter 2:24)

10. I uproot every tree of infirmity my heavenly Father has not planted in my life causing me increased errors or accidents, in the name of Jesus (Matthew 3:10)

11. Symptoms of insomnia and sleeplessness waiting to manifest at a later date in my life, wither and die now, in the name of Jesus[8] (Matthew 15:13)

Prayer Against Barrenness and Other Pregnancy Related Issues

<u>Scripture Reading</u>: 1 Samuel 1:1-2, 9-20; Genesis 25:21; Isaiah 54:1; Genesis 29:31

<u>Memory Verse/Confession</u>: Psalm 113:9

> *"He grants the barren woman a home, like a joyful mother of children. Praise the LORD!"*

<u>Explanation</u>:

The issue of barrenness or inability to get pregnant can be very traumatic because women are created with wombs and have been blessed by God to bring life into the world. Therefore, these prayers are very important to those who are having challenges getting pregnant.

THEME: WILL YOU BE MADE WHOLE?

1. Damage to my ovaries and uterus working against my ability to get pregnant, be healed immediately, in the name of Jesus (Psalm 127:3-6)
2. Hormonal issues causing me problems with my ovulation that may be blocking conception in my life, be emasculated by the blood of Jesus, in the name of Jesus (Genesis 18:10-15)
3. If God can move mountains, He can move barrenness, therefore I command every seed of barrenness in my body to wither and die now, in the name of Jesus (Matthew 19:26; Luke 1:37)

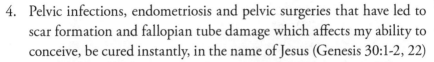

4. Pelvic infections, endometriosis and pelvic surgeries that have led to scar formation and fallopian tube damage which affects my ability to conceive, be cured instantly, in the name of Jesus (Genesis 30:1-2, 22)

5. Any cervical condition where the sperm is unable to successfully pass through the cervical canal because of abnormal mucus production or a prior cervical surgical procedure, be reversed completely, in the name of Jesus (1 Samuel 1:1-28)

6. I flush my womb of every pollution and complication by the blood of Jesus, in the name of Jesus (Revelations 12:11; Hebrews 12:24)

7. Abnormal anatomy of the uterus due to the presence of polyps and fibroids in my womb, release me by fire, in the name of Jesus (Hebrews 12:29; Judges 13:1-3)

8. God's Word declares 'Christ took my infirmities and bore my sicknesses', therefore I receive Christ's healing in my womb and receive grace to conceive, in the name of Jesus (Matthew 8:17-18)

9. Irregular menstrual cycles as well as complete stoppages in my menstrual flow causing me difficulty in getting pregnant, be healed now, in the name of Jesus (Isaiah 53:4-5)

10. Excessive bleeding, light menstrual flows and excessive cramps complicating my ability to conceive, be repaired by the Holy Ghost, in the name of Jesus (Acts 10:38)

11. Lord, deliver me from successive miscarriages and unintended abortions working against conception in my life, in the name of Jesus (Obadiah 1:17; 2 Timothy 4:18)

12. Any chronic illnesses, like diabetes, thyroid problems, or hypertension causing me inability to conceive, be reversed instantly, in the name of Jesus (2 Chronicles 7:13-14)

13. Any history of sexually transmitted diseases that may have caused infections, inflammation and blockage of the fallopian tubes, making pregnancy either impossible or putting me at risk for ectopic pregnancy, be healed by the antibiotic in the blood of Jesus, in the name of Jesus[9] (Genesis 11:30; Deuteronomy 7:14)

Healing From Tumors, Boils & Skin Diseases

<u>Scripture Reading</u>: Matthew 9:12; Isaiah 3:17; 2 Kings 5:27; 2 Samuel 12:15; Leviticus 15:1-33

<u>Memory Verse/Confession</u>: 2 Kings 20:7

"Then Isaiah said, "Take a lump of figs." So they took and laid *it* on the boil, and he recovered."

<u>Explanation</u>:

The issue of tumors, boils and skin diseases can be very devastating. These illnesses are most often an outward manifestation of an internal blood related problem. The prayers contained below will help us effectively deal with any of these situations.

HEAL ME LORD, AND I WILL BE HEALED

1. Any hidden tumor in my body manifesting as pancreatic cancer, receive fire and melt immediately, in the name of Jesus (Hebrews 12:29)
2. Lung tumors causing coughing, shortness of breath and chest pain in my life, be healed instantly, in the name of Jesus (Acts 19:12)
3. I address every blood infection and pollution causing recurring boils on different parts of my body by the antibiotic power in the blood of Jesus, in the name of Jesus (Revelations 12:11; Hebrews 12:24)

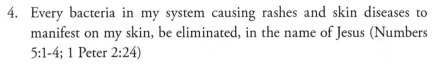
4. Every bacteria in my system causing rashes and skin diseases to manifest on my skin, be eliminated, in the name of Jesus (Numbers 5:1-4; 1 Peter 2:24)

5. Tumors of the colon causing weight loss, diarrhea, constipation, iron deficiency anemia and blood in the stool, vanish completely, in the name of Jesus (Matthew 8:1-3)

6. Symptoms of chills, fatigue, fever, loss of appetite, discomfort, night sweats and weight loss that are the result of tumors, release me now, in the name of Jesus (Isaiah 10:27)

7. Brain and spinal cord tumors manifesting as headaches, nausea, vomiting, blurred vision, balance problems, personality or behavior changes, compression of the nerves, seizures and weight loss, be healed by the stripes of Jesus, in the name of Jesus (Isaiah 53:4-5)

8. Tumors in any part of my brain causing me pressure inside the skull also known as intracranial pressure, melt be fire and the blood of Jesus, in the name of Jesus (Deuteronomy 4:24; Hebrews 12:24)

9. Any boil growing on any part of my body, I extinguish you with your accompanying symptoms, in the name of Jesus (Nahum 1:13)

10. Lord, deliver and heal me totally of tumors, boils and skin diseases, in the name of Jesus[10] (Obadiah 1:17)

Destiny-Molding Prayers & Exhortations

These are carefully selected prayers for all of life's battles and situations. They provide direction, as well as inspiration and guidance on how to pray regarding different aspects of human existence.

I Will Not Be Confused

<u>Scripture Reading</u>: Psalm 119:34; John 16:13; 2 Timothy 3:16-17; 1 Corinthians 13:12

<u>Memory Verse/Confession</u>: 1 Corinthians 14:33

> *"For God is not the author of confusion but of peace, as in all the churches of the saints."*

<u>Explanation</u>:

Confusion creates a state of mental disarray in which the individual is overwhelmed or largely at a loss as to what to do, or how to proceed. Our God is an all-knowing God (Job 37:14-15), who not only is and knows the beginning from the end (Revelations 22:13), but also is able to reveal, direct, control and alter the outcome of our lives and aspirations (Daniel 2:20-22). There is nothing too difficult for Him to do (Jeremiah 32:26-27). As you pray these prayers, God will bring His light and clarity into every dark area and situation in your life (Psalm 119:105, 130).

THEME: RELEASE FROM THE SPIRIT OF CONFUSION

1. I refuse to be confused, for God my Father is not the author of confusion, in Jesus name
2. (1 Corinthians 14:33; 2 Timothy 2:7)
3. Father Lord, release the arrow of confusion into the camp of my enemies, that they may fight themselves and destroy themselves, in Jesus name (Isaiah 49:26; II Chronicles 20:20-25)

4. Holy Spirit, give me the spirit of understanding and clarity in all my undertakings, in Jesus name (John 16:13; Psalm 119:125)

5. Lord, confuse and turn the counsel of my Ahithophel(s) to foolishness, in Jesus name (2 Samuel 15:31)

6. Let the peace that surpasses all understanding and the calmness of God reign in my heart, mind and soul, in the name of Jesus (Hebrews 12:14; Isaiah 26:3)

7. Every spirit of fear sponsoring confusion in my life, release my destiny, in the name of Jesus (2 Timothy 1:7)

8. Pressures overwhelming me to the point of confusion, loose your grip over my life, in the name of Jesus (Philippians 4:6-7)

9. I break out of circles of confusion holding me captive, in the name of Jesus (Obadiah 1:17; Nahum 1:13)

10. Every spiritual label the devil is using to put my life in disarray, be blotted out by the blood of Jesus, in the name of Jesus (Colossians 2:14)

11. Any demonic word spoken over me to turn my life upside down, I overturn and reverse you, in the name of Jesus (Isaiah 54:17B)

Thou Shall Not Covet

Scripture Reading: Luke 12:15-21; 1 John 2:15-17; 1 Timothy 6:10; Exodus 20:17; Ephesians 5:3

Memory Verse/Confession: Colossians 3:5 (NLT)

> *"So put to death the sinful, earthly things lurking within you. Have nothing to do with sexual immorality, impurity, lust, and evil desires. Don't be greedy, for a greedy person is an idolater, worshiping the things of this world."*

Explanation:

God detests covetousness because it makes us focus on material things when we ought to be focusing on Him. We are created in God's image to fellowship with Him, and provision is included in the package. So the things we chase after or worry about are things the Creator has freely given to us (1 Corinthians 2:12; II Corinthians 9:10-11). The secret to living above covetousness is provided in Matthew 6:33 that tells us to seek first the kingdom and His righteousness, and all other things shall be added to us.

THEME: DEALING WITH THE SPIRIT OF COVETOUSNESS

1. O Lord, help me to be satisfied with all you have blessed me with, for Godliness with contentment is great, in the name of Jesus (Hebrews 13:5; 1 Timothy 6:6)

2. I refuse to receive and be selfish, but rather choose to be a conduit for God's blessings to others; for it is more blessed to give than to receive, in Jesus name (Proverbs 21:26; Hebrews 13:5)

3. Holy Spirit, take away from me an envious eye and covetous heart, in the name of Jesus (1 John 2:16-17; Colossians 3:5)

4. I receive wisdom to understand that the value of a man is not measured by possessions, in the name of Jesus (Luke 12:15; Ephesians 5:5)

5. I reject the spirit that hoards, for there is one who withholds more than is necessary, and it leads to poverty, in Jesus name (Proverbs 11:24; Romans 13:9)

6. Anything within me that only wants to grab and keep, release me and perish, in Jesus name (Mark 7:20-23; Matthew 16:26)

7. Every strange fire of covetousness burning in my heart, I extinguish you completely, in the name of Jesus (Leviticus 10:1-2 KJV; 2 Peter 2:12-16)

8. My soul is more important than my daily provision, so as I have trusted God with my soul, I also trust Him for my daily needs, in the name of Jesus (Proverbs 3:5-6; Isaiah 40:31)

9. Holy Spirit, deliver me from the love and fascination with money and material possessions, in the name of Jesus (Proverbs 23:4-5; 1 Timothy 6:6-12)

10. I receive grace and understanding to be more concerned with winning souls and kingdom profit than to be preoccupied with money and gaining material wealth, in the name of Jesus (Proverbs 11:30; Luke 9:25)

Overcoming Crisis

<u>Scripture Reading</u>: 1 Timothy 2:1-2; James 4:1-2; Acts 1:7-8; Luke 21:36, Matthew 24:6

<u>Memory Verse/Confession</u>: Psalm 34: 17-20 (NLT)

> *"The LORD hears his people when they call to him for help. He rescues them from all their troubles. The LORD is close to the brokenhearted; he rescues those whose spirits are crushed. The righteous person faces many troubles, but the LORD comes to the rescue each time. For the LORD protects the bones of the righteous; not one of them is broken!"*

<u>Explanation</u>:

We live in a world that is largely imperfect because of the fall of man and the damage done by sin. It is true we have been given dominion over the earth, but the ability to exercise that dominion is constantly under attack by various enemy powers. While these attacks sometimes manifest as crises, I want to assure you that we are victorious because our Lord and Elder Brother Jesus is the Master of Crisis and has led principalities and powers captive, making a public and triumphant show of them (Colossians 2:15).

THEME: MASTER OF CRISIS

1. I refuse to be stranded or afflicted, in the name of Jesus (Psalm 91:5-8; Psalm 46:1-3)

2. Jesus Christ is the Master of crisis, so I will not be overcome by crises, in the name of Jesus (2 Corinthians 12:9; Mark 4:35-41)

3. I receive strength to mount up with wings as an eagle over the winds of any crisis blowing against me, in the name of Jesus (Isaiah 40:28-31)

4. O Lord, deliver me from every ungodly pattern of recurring crises, in Jesus name (Nahum 1:9; Isaiah 10:27)

5. I hide myself in the secret place of the Most High, that I may abide under the shadow of the Almighty, in Jesus name (Psalm 91:1)

6. The Lord will defend me and my loved ones from all forms of crises because He loves us with an undying love, in the name of Jesus (Isaiah 31:5; Psalm 103:6; Jeremiah 31:3)

7. My Father and My God, keep me as the apple of Your eye far above the reach of principalities and powers, in the name of Jesus (Zechariah 2:8; Deuteronomy 32:9-11)

8. Wall of fire of protection of the Most High God, surround and protect me from the works of darkness, in the name of Jesus (Zechariah 2:5)

9. Generational curses sponsoring affliction and crisis in my life, be broken by fire, in the name of Jesus (Galatians 3:13; Colossians 2:14)

10. I am too protected to be in crisis and too blessed to be stranded, in the name of Jesus (2 Corinthians 4:8-9; John 14:1-31)

Abundant Life

<u>Scripture Reading</u>: John 3:14-17; Jeremiah 29:11; Matthew 6:33; Romans 15:13; Isaiah 58:11

<u>Memory Verse/Confession</u>: John 10:10 (AMP)

> *"The thief comes only in order to steal and kill and destroy. I came that they may have and enjoy life, and have it in abundance (to the full, till it overflows)."*

<u>Explanation</u>:

The grace of God is responsible for the salvation we receive as the key to the abundant life we can enjoy in Christ. Abundant life not only guarantees a wonderful life here on earth, but also ensures we get to spend eternity with God. These prayers are intended to make sure we do not miss out on all that rightly belongs to us.

THEME: LIVING LIFE TO THE FULLEST

1. Christ has come that I might have life and have it more abundantly, and I receive the fullness of that life now, in Jesus name (John 10:10)
2. The Bible says the Jordan overflows its banks all harvest, so I command my Jordan to perpetually overflow its banks, in the name of Jesus (Joshua 3:15)
3. I call forth abundance from the east, west, north and south, in the name of Jesus (Job 22:28 – KJV)

4. I disappoint every plan or device hindering abundance in my life, in the name of Jesus (Job 5:12

5. Let the glory of the former, present, and latter house, collide in my life, to bring about an explosion of abundance, in the name of Jesus (Haggai 2:9)

6. I receive the enrichment of God's fertilizer to enrich the soil in the garden of my life, in the name of Jesus (Romans 9:15-16)

7. Lord, identify and destroy all little foxes spoiling the vine of my life and harvest, in the name of Jesus (Songs of Solomon 2:15)

8. Father Lord, You are the Lord that daily loads me with benefits; manifest Your glory in my life, in the name of Jesus (Psalm 68:19)

9. Lord, You are the God who can bring money out of the mouth of a fish, perform the impossible in my life and situations, in the name of Jesus (Matthew 27:24-27)

10. Father Lord, You're the Lord who gives us power to get wealth, cause my financial heavens to open for my blessing, in the name of Jesus (Deuteronomy 8:18)

Alertness and Attentiveness

<u>Scripture Reading</u>: Matthew 13:13-16; Luke 21:36 (NLT); Ephesians 6:18; Matthew 24:44

<u>Memory Verse/Confession</u>: 1 Peter 5:8-9

> *"Be sober, be vigilant; because your adversary the devil walks about like a roaring lion, seeking whom he may devour. Resist him, steadfast in the faith, knowing that the same sufferings are experienced by your brotherhood in the world."*

<u>Explanation</u>:

Alertness and vigilance are necessary in order for us to have sensitivity in any given situation. The truth is that if we're not alert and sensitive in life, we're not able to take advantage of all it has to offer. Therefore, paying attention to detail is the first step to being able to understand and properly utilize an opportunity.

THEME: PAYING ATTENTION TO DETAIL

1. God has not given me the spirit of fear, but of power, love, and a sound mind, so I decree my mind is sound and alert, in Jesus name (2 Timothy 1:7)
2. I receive the mind of Christ to effectively do the will of God, in the name of Jesus (Philippians 2:5; 1 Corinthians 2:16)
3. Like Jesus, I set my face like a flint on kingdom priorities, and decree my focus cannot be broken, in the name of Jesus (Luke 9:51)

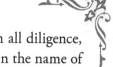

4. Father Lord, grant me the grace to keep my heart with all diligence, so I can properly master and control the issues of life, in the name of Jesus (Proverbs 4:23)

5. Holy Spirit, help me to be quick to listen, slow to speak, and dead to anger, in the name of Jesus (James 1:19)

6. You my soul, cease to wander all over the place, and go back to your resting place, in the name of Jesus (Psalm 116:7)

7. I break the stronghold of the vagabond spirit that causes my mind to wander and be restless, in the name (Job 1:6-7, Job 2:1-2; Philippians 4:6-7)

8. I receive the power to continually be focused, alert and prayerful, in the name of Jesus (Matthew 26:41)

9. I prophesy upon my life, that as Jesus was focused on the cross and succeeded, I will focus on seeking the Lord and his righteousness and succeed, in the name of Jesus (Luke 9:51; Matthew 6:33)

10. I receive the grace for divine alertness and concentration, in Jesus name (Psalm 119:105; Matthew 24:4; 1 Timothy 4:16-11- NIV)

The Blessings of the Covenant

<u>Scripture Reading</u>: Deuteronomy 28:1-13; Proverbs 10:22; Philippians 4:19; James 1:17

<u>Memory Verse/Confession</u>: Isaiah 60:15-16

> *"Whereas you have been forsaken and hated, so that no one went through you, I will make you an eternal excellence, a joy of many generations. You shall drink the milk of the gentiles, and milk the breast of kings; you shall know that I the Lord, Am your Savior and your Redeemer, the mighty One of Jacob."*

<u>Explanation</u>:

God has put before us life and death. Life in Christ is the key to blessings, while a life of spiritual death (earthly and eternal spiritual separation from God) carries curses (Deuteronomy 30:19). So choose life and the blessings of God will pursue and overtake you.

THEME: DESTINED TO PROSPER

1. Christ died poor that I might be rich, therefore I access and claim all the riches of His glory and grace, in the name of Jesus (2 Corinthians 8:9)
2. I decree I am the head and not the tail, I am always above, and not beneath; I lend to nations and do not borrow, in the name of Jesus (Deuteronomy 28:12-13)

3. I receive the wisdom of the Holy Spirit to know the things that have been freely given to me by God, in the name of Jesus (1 Corinthians 2:12)

4. I appropriate the fullness of the blessings of God that make rich and add no sorrow, in the name of Jesus (Proverbs 10:22)

5. I agree with God's Word that I'm blessed in the city and in the country, and I'm blessed in my going out and my coming in, in the name of Jesus (Deuteronomy 28:3,6)

6. I receive the locational grace and anointing of the Holy Spirit, to be at the right place, at the right time, doing the right thing, for the right results, in the name of Jesus (Romans 8:14; Isaiah 30:21)

7. Like the sons of Issachar, I receive the wisdom and discernment to understand my times and seasons, in the name of Jesus (1 Chronicles 12:32)

8. I command the Holy Spirit to magnetize my divine helpers to me from the east, west, north and south, in the name of Jesus (Isaiah 46:11; 1 Kings 17:1-6, 8-16)

9. O Lord, command Your blessings on my storehouses, and in everything I do, and bless me in the land You have given me, in the name of Jesus (Deuteronomy 28:8)

10. Holy Spirit, as You open up doors of expansion to me, help me to taste and see that the Lord is good, in Jesus name (Isaiah 54:2-5; Psalm 34:8)

The Blood Advantage

<u>Scripture Reading</u>: Hebrews 9:11-28; John 19:33-34; Acts 5:28; 1 John 5:6-7; Hebrews 10:3-14

<u>Memory Verse/Confession</u>: Revelations 12:11

> *"And they overcame him by the blood of the Lamb and by the word of their testimony, and they did not love their lives to the death."*

<u>Explanation</u>:

The Blood of Jesus is the blood of the eternal sacrifice. A blood that is both spotless and sinless. It has the purity and power to cleanse and renew. The blood of the Lamb of God is an overcoming and better speaking blood. It is the only blood that was adequate to answer and settle the sin question once and for all, and open the gates of grace so we could have full access to redemption. A proper understanding of the power of the blood positions us to take advantage of its benefits in our prayers.

THEME: THE BETTER SPEAKING BLOOD

1. I command the overcoming power in the blood of Jesus to begin to overcome every attack and challenge I'm currently encountering, in the name of Jesus (Revelations 12:11)
2. Let the superior speaking power in the blood of Jesus, silence every contrary voice speaking against my life, in the name of Jesus (Heb. 12:24)

3. I cover myself with the blood of Jesus, and declare my life free from bewitchment, manipulation, and attacks, in the name of Jesus (1 Peter 1:8-19)

4. I drink and transfuse myself with the blood of Jesus for cleansing, healing, and deliverance, in the name of Jesus (Revelations 1:5; Isaiah 53:4-5)

5. I draw the bloodline of the Lord Jesus Christ around my family, job, finances, and health, for maximum protection, in the name of Jesus (Exodus 12:13)

6. Favor in the blood of Jesus connect me to men and women you have chosen to bless me, in the name of Jesus (Psalm 102:13)

7. Wherever contrary voices are speaking against me, I command the blood of Jesus to defend and fight for me, in the name of Jesus (Hebrews 12:24)

8. Let the power and anointing in the blood of Jesus locate and dismiss every ungodly gathering against my wellbeing, in the name of Jesus (Isaiah 54:14; Revelations 12:11)

9. Let the blood with which Jesus saved and redeemed me from eternal damnation begin to speak up for me anywhere my name is being mentioned for evil, in the name of Jesus (1 John 3:8B)

10. I take refuge in the protection of the blood of Jesus, in the name of Jesus (Hebrews 2:14; Hebrews 10:12)

The Spirit of Boldness

<u>Scripture Reading</u>: Hebrews 10:19-22; Acts 4:13; Acts 4:23-31; Ephesians 6:19; Hebrews 13:6

<u>Memory Verse/Confession</u>: Proverbs 28:1

> *"The wicked flee when no one pursues, but the righteous are bold as a lion"*

<u>Explanation</u>:

The spirit of boldness is necessary to live a victorious life in Christ. Those that have fully yielded to the leading and empowering grace of the Holy Spirit, also enjoy the boldness that He enables them to walk in. The prayers you are about to pray have the potential to increase your boldness, so you can be the best you can be for Him.

THEME: COURAGE FOR DIVINE EXPLOITS

1. The Bible says God has not given me the spirit of timidity, I therefore claim the spirit of boldness, in the name of Jesus (2 Timothy 1:7)
2. As the Lord instructed Joshua to be bold and courageous, I receive the anointing of courage and boldness, in the name of Jesus (Joshua 1:6-7)
3. Let God be true in my life and circumstances and everything else a liar, in the name of Jesus (Romans 3:3-4)
4. I refuse to focus on the greatness of my challenges, but rather turn my attention to the omnipotence of my God, in Jesus name (Numbers 13:31-33; Matthew 19:21)

5. I agree with God's Word that I am able to go up and possess my inheritance, and receive boldness to run towards my goliath, in the name of Jesus (Deuteronomy 1:8; Numbers 13:30; 1 Samuel 17:48-52)

6. My Father is the Lion of the tribe of Judah, therefore I receive boldness to confront and defeat every counterfeit lion, in the name of Jesus (Revelations 5:5; 1 Peter 5:8)

7. The Lord will keep me in perfect peace, because my heart is dependent on Him, and I trust Him totally, in the name of Jesus (Isaiah 26:3)

8. Holy Spirit, anoint me with boldness, in the name of Jesus (Psalm 138:3)

9. Oh Lord, give me a heart of courage, to be bold in season and out of season, in the name of Jesus (Joshua 1:9)

10. I decree I am strong in the Lord, and in the power of His might, in the name of Jesus (Ephesians 6:10)

My Turn To Walk Down The Aisle

<u>Scripture Reading</u>: Matthew 7:24-29, Isaiah 49:24-26; Genesis 2:18-25; Proverbs 4:18

<u>Memory Verse/Confession</u>: Isaiah 10:27

> *"And it shall come to pass in that day, that his burden shall be taken away from off thy shoulder, and the yoke from off thy neck, and the yoke shall be destroyed because of the anointing."*

<u>Explanation</u>:

Marriage is a consummation of love, not only of Christ with His Church, but also between man and woman. In this union differences are put aside for two to become one, so they can fully reflect the image of Christ. However, because of the carnal nature of man, decisions have to be made through prayers and in accordance with the will of God.

THEME: IT IS NOT GOOD FOR MAN TO BE ALONE

1. Lord, reveal to me Your will for me in marriage, in the name of Jesus (Daniel 2:22; Deuteronomy 29:29)
2. Holy Spirit, give me the sensitivity and discernment to successfully locate and identify my life partner, in Jesus name (Genesis 2:18-25; Proverbs 18:22)
3. Lord, help me get rid of the idols in my heart, to enable me get clear directions for my marriage, in Jesus name (Ezekiel 14:1-5)

4. Holy Ghost, magnetize my life partner to me, in Jesus name (Isaiah 46:11; Job 23:14)
5. I break myself free from the yoke of marital delay, in the name of Jesus (Ezekiel 12:21-28)
6. I receive uncommon divine favor to be discovered and chosen, in Jesus name (Psalm 5:12)
7. Any mark of rejection delaying my marital breakthrough, be erased by the blood of Jesus, in Jesus name (Colossians 2:14; Revelations 12:11)
8. Foundational chains that have been used to tie down my marriage, break and release my marriage instantly, in Jesus name (Nahum 1:13)
9. Any pattern of marital delay and failure affecting the women/men in my family, release my destiny by fire, in Jesus name (Obadiah 1:17)
10. As I celebrated with others over their weddings, people will celebrate with me this year, in the name of Jesus (Isaiah 61:7)

Prayers Against Daydreaming

Scripture Reading: Proverbs 4:23; Proverbs 23:7A; Ephesians 2:2-3A; Ephesians 6:12; 1 Peter 5:8-9

Memory Verse/Confession: Philippians 4:8

> *"Finally, brethren, whatever things are true, whatever things are noble, whatever things are just, whatever things are pure, whatever things are lovely, whatever things are of good report, if there is any virtue and if there is anything praiseworthy—meditate on these things."*

Explanation:

We have a tendency to daydream because God put in us the potential to dream. The ability to dream is meant to help us connect with the supernatural since we are able to receive messages from God (Matthew 1:20-21), as well as sense attacks from the enemy in the course of our dream lives (Matthew 13:25). But beyond this obvious advantage, God has also given us the capacity to dream up a future and see ourselves by faith in our land of promise. The adverse side to this is when this process is not carefully mastered and implemented; it could drift into periods of aimless daydreaming where the mind wonders without purpose. These prayers are meant to combat this problem.

THEME: LIVING IN LIGHT OF REALITY

1. O Lord, help me recognize the difference between daydreaming and reality, and to stay alert and on the part of reality, in the name of Jesus (Proverbs 4:7; Isaiah 48:17)

2. I refuse to daydream, but choose to focus and be serious about life's opportunities and challenges, in the name of Jesus (James 1:19; 1 Chronicles 12:32)

3. Let the spirit of leisure and laziness that causes me to daydream depart from my life now, in Jesus name (Proverbs 20:13; Proverbs 10:5; Proverbs 24:30-34; Ephesians 5:15-16)

4. Holy Spirit, remove from my life the spirit of slumber and create in me the love for diligence in my work, in the name of Jesus (Proverbs 6:9-11; Proverbs 10:4; 1 Timothy 5:8)

5. Father Lord, enable me to recognize and properly maximize my divine potentials, rather than living in lalaland, in the name of Jesus (Isaiah 40:31)

6. Arrows fired into my life to make me sluggish and unresponsive to opportunities that will better my life, jump out and locate your sender now, in the name of Jesus (Psalm 18:44-45)

7. Holy Spirit, may I not daydream and worry about what I could have achieved, instead of taking advantage of what life has to offer right now, in the name of Jesus (Philippians 3:13-15)

8. My Lord & My God, let Your light of vision, faith and aspiration never grow dim in my heart, in the name of Jesus (Habakkuk 2:2-3; Hebrews 11:6)

9. Farther Lord, help to see the way You see, so I can aspire and succeed in like manner, in the name of Jesus (Jeremiah 1:11-12)

10. Witchcraft inspired daydreaming being used to slow me down, be exposed and disgraced, in the name of Jesus (Numbers 23:23)

11. Every good thing I have lost through daydreaming, I take them back instantly, in the name of Jesus (1 Samuel 30:8)

I Will Not Die But Live

Scripture Reading: Psalm 118:17-18; Psalm 91:16; Isaiah 28:18; Psalm 50:15

Memory Verse/Confession: Job 5:26

"You shall come to the grave at a full age, as a sheaf of grain ripens in its season."

Explanation:

The Bible promises us a life of victory here on earth and an eternity with God our Father, and our Lord Jesus Christ. One of the benefits of the victory we are supposed to enjoy during our sojourn on earth is the incentive of a long and productive life. God may have promised us a lengthy and abundant life, but it's also only in Him we can fulfill that life. As you worship and seek to please Him daily, He is obligated to make sure His Words become flesh in your life and that you and your loved ones live to declare His works in the land of the living.

THEME: DESTROYING THE POWERS OF THE GRAVE

1. Death and life are in the power of my tongue, and I love it, so I eat the fruit by rejecting untimely death and choosing life, in Jesus name (Proverbs 18:21; Deuteronomy 30:19)
2. I break the backbone of the spirit of death, because it is written that I shall not die, but live, and declare the works of the Lord, in Jesus name (Psalm 118:17)

3. O Lord, help me to come to the grave at a full age, as a sheaf of grain ripens in its season, in the name of Jesus (Job 5:26)

4. I will live to a ripe old age because I know Who I've trusted, that He is able to keep that which I've entrusted to Him till the time of Christ, in the name of Jesus (1 Chronicles 29:26-28; 2 Timothy 1:12)

5. Father Lord, close the gates of premature, sudden, and untimely death against my family and I, in the name of Jesus (Revelations 3:7; John 10:7)

6. King of kings, You have the power to kill and make alive; protect and preserve my life and the life of my loved ones continually, in the name of Jesus (Deuteronomy 32:39)

7. Wicked traps of calamity and death set for me and my loved ones, locate and consume the life of those who set you, in the name of Jesus (Psalm 7:15; Psalm 35:8; Psalm 57:6)

8. Every covenant entered into with the powers of the grave to swallow my life, fail and backfire now, in the name of Jesus (Isaiah 28:15-18; Psalm 18:1-20)

9. Witchcraft burial done to bury my health and glory, be neutralized by the blood of Jesus, in the name of Jesus (Revelations 12:11)

10. Satanic grave diggers digging graves to bury me, and satanic carpenters constructing coffins to swallow my life, enter into your coffins and graves and be buried alive, in the name of Jesus (Proverbs 11:8; 2 Thessalonians 1:6; Revelations 13:10)

Arresting The Spirit of Deceit

<u>Scripture Reading</u>: 2 Corinthians 11:3; 1 Peter 3:10; Colossians 3:9-10; Jeremiah 9:6

<u>Memory Verse/Confession</u>: Proverbs 20:17

> *"Bread gained by deceit is sweet to a man, but afterward his mouth will be filled with gravel."*

<u>Explanation:</u>

The Lord hates deceit because He is a God of truth who does not have the capacity to lie, nor behold lies or iniquity (Habakkuk 1:13). We are not only created in His image, but have become the righteousness of God in Christ Jesus (2 Corinthians 5:21); and as such we have been given to the power to live holy just as He is holy. The prayers in this topic will help you live a life of truth.

THEME: I WILL NOT DECEIVE OR BE DECEIVED

1. O Lord, expose and disgrace every agent of deceit working against my life, in Jesus name (Psalm 38:12-16)
2. Father Lord, let your light expose any darkness or falsehood in my life, in the name of Jesus (Psalm 5:6; Daniel 2:22)
3. Lord Jesus, reveal the truth to me and help me to practice that truth, that the truth may set me free completely, in the name of Jesus (John 8:32; 36)

4. Holy Spirit, expose and frustrate any attempt to deceive me, in the name of Jesus (Psalm 120:2)

5. I indentify and resist every scheme of deception aimed at defrauding me, in the name of Jesus (Proverbs 6:16-19)

6. O Lord, because You hate deceit, expose and disgrace every deceiver in my circle of friends, in the name of Jesus (Psalm 101:7; Proverbs 26:24-25)

7. Father Lord, identify and discipline all false prophets and ministers using the Bible to deceive Your people, in the name of Jesus (Romans 16:18; Colossians 2:8; Psalm 36:1-4)

8. Holy Spirit, search my heart continually and deliver me from the tendency to be deceitful, in the name of Jesus (Jeremiah 17:9; Proverbs 4:23)

9. I pull down the foundation and building stones of lies in my life and the life of my loved ones, in the name of Jesus (Proverbs 19:9; Mark 7:20-23)

10. Any wicked company that have set out to destroy me through lies and falsehood, receive divine embarrassment and disgrace, in the name of Jesus (Psalm 10:7; Psalm 43:1)

The Power of Consecration

<u>Scripture Reading</u>: 1 Corinthians 6:20; 1Peter 2:9; Romans 6:13; Romans 6:16; 2 Corinthians 9:3-5

<u>Memory verse/Confession</u>: Psalm 51:17

> *"The sacrifices of God are a broken spirit, A broken and a contrite heart – These, O God, You will not despise."*

<u>Explanation</u>:

God is the one who sanctifies, but for that process to be initiated and work properly, we have to consecrate ourselves. Consecration is that art of setting oneself apart from the world and its attractions, while turning to the Lord for His sanctification and use.

THEME: I CONSECRATE MYSELF TO YOU, LORD

1. O Lord, purge and purify me as gold and silver, that I may offer to You, an offering in righteousness, in Jesus name (2 Timothy 2:20-21)
2. Holy Spirit, circumcise my heart, that the meditations of my heart and the sacrifice of my lips may be acceptable to You, in the name of Jesus (Psalm 19:14)
3. Blood of Jesus, wash me from inside out and remove every blemish from my life, in Jesus name (Revelations 12:11; Ephesians 5:22)
4. Father Lord, sanctify me as I consecrate myself to You, in Jesus name (Leviticus 20:7; Joshua 3:5)

5. Lord Jesus, break me, re-mold me, and use me effectively for your glory, in Jesus name (Isaiah 57:15)

6. Lord, I present myself a living sacrifice, holy and acceptable to You, in the name of Jesus (Romans 12:1)

7. O Lord, create in me a clean heart and renew a right spirit within me, in the name of Jesus (Psalm 51:10)

8. Father Lord, identify and get rid of the little foxes spoiling the vine of my heart, in the name of Jesus (Songs of Solomon 2:15)

9. I refuse to be conformed to this world, and rather I choose to be transformed by the renewing of my mind by God's Word, in the name of Jesus (Romans 12:2; Hebrews 4:12-13)

10. Holy Spirit, position me for good works that bring glory to Your name alone, in the name of Jesus (Ephesians 2:10)

The Spirit of Jealousy

Scripture Reading: Proverbs 10:12; Songs of Solomon 8:6-7; Proverbs 14:30; Romans 13:13

Memory Verse/Confession: James 3:14-16

> *"But if you have bitter envy and self-seeking in your hearts, do not boast and lie against the truth. This wisdom does not descend from above, but is earthly, sensual, and demonic. For where envy and self-seeking exist, confusion and every evil thing are there."*

Explanation:

Jealousy is the same as envy, and points to discontent with the way God has made us. It is being envious of someone else for who they are or what they have. The Bible frowns at jealousy and flat out commands us not to be jealous (James 3:14-16; Exodus 20:17). These prayers are anointed to help us overcome jealousy.

THEME: POWER OVER THE SPIRIT OF JEALOUSY

1. I was created unique, there are no two of me, so I refuse to be jealous, in the name of Jesus (Ezekiel 16:42)
2. Let the spirit of envy release my destiny, in the name of Jesus (1 Peter 2:11; Ephesians 4:1-2)
3. I arrest the spirit of covetousness and discontent that causes me to be jealous, in the name of Jesus (James 4:1-3)

4. O Lord, take away from me every root of bitterness and envy, in the name of Jesus (Philippians 2:3; James 3:15-16)

5. Father Lord, give me a generous heart that rejoices at the victory of others, in the name of Jesus (Psalm 37:1-3)

6. Jealousy is a destroyer, so I refuse to have any part of it, in the name of Jesus (Proverbs 27:4; Proverbs 6:34)

7. Holy Spirit, deliver me from carnality and every fleshy conduct, in the name of Jesus (1 Corinthians 3:3; John 8:32)

8. O Lord, search my heart and cleanse me of every root of envy and jealousy, in the name of Jesus (James 3:14-16; Proverbs 4:23)

9. Father Lord, help me to love and not yield to the temptation to pay back evil for evil, in the name of Jesus (Romans 12:21; Galatians 5:14-15)

10. I receive patience and perseverance to accommodate those who offend or irritate me, in the name of Jesus (Colossians 1:11; Hebrews 10:36)

Lust

Scripture Reading: Colossians 3:5; 1 Peter 2:11; John 14:15; Hebrews 13:4; Psalm 119:9-10

Memory Verse/Confession: Job 31:1 (NIV)

"I made a covenant with my eyes not to look lustfully at a young woman."

Explanation:

Lust is a strong inward sexual desire or appetite, which manifests itself in negative sexual behavior. The Bible is vehemently opposed to such thoughts and desires and the attitudes and behaviors that emanate from them. These prayers are meant to enable us to live and overcome the problem of lust.

THEME: RELEASING YOURSELF FROM THE SPIRIT OF LUST

1. I release my destiny from the hold of the spirit of lust, in the name of Jesus (Romans 8:6)
2. Every arrow of the spirit of lust fired into my life, be neutralized by fire, in the name of Jesus (Psalm 101:3)
3. Father Lord, help me to overcome the works of the flesh, in the name of Jesus (Galatians 5:19-21, 16-18)
4. Let every agent of the enemy that has been anointed with the spirit of lust to pull me down, be exposed and disgraced, in the name of Jesus (Isaiah 54:17; Romans 13:14)

5. Holy Spirit, take control of my thought life, and use it for Your glory, in the name of Jesus (Psalm 86:11)

6. I receive grace to flee from the sin of lust and sexual immorality, in the name of Jesus (1 Corinthians 6:18, 1 Corinthians 6:13)

7. Father Lord, fill me with Your Word that the temple of my life might be a suitable place for the Holy Spirit to dwell, in the name of Jesus (Colossians 3:16; 1 Corinthians 6:19-20)

8. I receive the spirit of self control, to live above lust and sexual temptation, in the name of Jesus (1 Thessalonians 4:3-5)

9. Lord, I enter into covenant with my heart and eyes that I will not meditate or look lustfully at a woman/man, in Jesus name (Matthew 5:28; Job 31:1)

10. I choose to be led by the Word and Spirit of God, rather than be controlled by the lust and vanity of life, in the name of Jesus (1 John 2:16; 2 Timothy 2:22)

Prayers For Children

<u>Scripture Reading</u>: Genesis 18:19; Genesis33:5; Psalm 113:9; 2 Timothy 3:14-15

<u>Memory verse/Confession</u>: James 1:17

> *"Every good gift and every perfect gift is from above, and comes down from the Father of lights, with whom there is no variation or shadow of turning."*

<u>Explanation</u>:

Children are a gift from God to humanity and as such matters relating to them ought to be handled with the utmost care. One of the reasons God gave Eve to Adam is to produce godly seed (Malachi 2:15). The Bible says children are a heritage from the Lord and the fruit of the womb is a reward (Psalm 127:3). The prayers contained in this program are for our children.

THEME: CREATED FOR SIGNS AND WONDERS

1. My children and I were created for signs and wonders and will manifest signs and wonders in every area of our lives, in the name of Jesus (Isaiah 8:18)
2. I decree the wisdom of the ancients and the wisdom that surpasses that of their teachers upon my children, in the name of Jesus (Psalm 119:99-100; Job 12:12)
3. I will not bury my children, but my children will bury me at a ripe old age, in the name of Jesus (Exodus 23:25-26; Psalm 91:16)

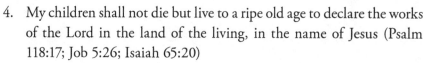

---

4. My children shall not die but live to a ripe old age to declare the works of the Lord in the land of the living, in the name of Jesus (Psalm 118:17; Job 5:26; Isaiah 65:20)

5. Every power assigned to kill or terminate life at infancy, you are not permitted to see or touch my children, in Jesus name (Matthew 2:16-18; Genesis 15:15)

6. I dedicate my children to the Lord Jesus Christ, to do with them as He pleases, in the name of Jesus (1 Samuel 1:11)

7. The Bible says the glory of the latter house shall surpass that of the former, therefore I prophesy that my children shall love the Lord more and be more successful than I, in the name of Jesus (Proverbs 4:18; Haggai 2:9)

8. I decree that my children are a gift and a solution to their generation and future generations, in the name of Jesus (Psalm 127:3-5)

9. I decree my children know their God, are strong, and shall do exploits, in the name of Jesus (Daniel 11:32)

10. I prophesy concerning my children's health, education, marriages, and careers, that they are blessed, and their names shall be mentioned in the corridors of power, in Jesus name (Isaiah 49:23; Isaiah 50:4; Deuteronomy 28:1-14)

11. My children are obedient and taught in the fear and admonition of the Lord, in Jesus name (Ephesians 6:1,4)

Master of Creativity

<u>Scripture Reading</u>: Galatians 6:4; 1 Corinthians 9:19-23; Ecclesiastes 1:9; 1 Corinthians 3:10

<u>Memory verse/Confession</u>: Exodus 35:31-32

> *"And He has filled him with the Spirit of God, in wisdom and understanding, in knowledge and all manner of workmanship, to design artistic works, to work in gold and silver and bronze."*

<u>Explanation</u>:

One of the gifts God has given to man is the gift of creativity. Man was created with the potential to rule over his world through creativity and by positively affecting his environment. This is why man has been responsible for creating new inventions after God created the earth and mankind. The prayers in this program are to bring out all the creative ability buried within you.

THEME: CREATIVITY RULES THE WORLD

1. Holy Spirit, anoint me with wisdom and ingenuity for inventive ideas and concepts, in the name of Jesus (Exodus 31:1-6)
2. Let every untapped creative potential residing in my life, be made manifest in the name of Jesus (Proverbs 22:29)
3. Let the grace of God to maximize my creative potentials be released upon me now, in the name of Jesus (Genesis 1:1-31)

4. Father Lord, help me to develop every raw creative ability You originally placed in me, so I can be a solution to my generation, in the name of Jesus (Genesis 1:27-28; Psalm 104:24)

5. O Lord, fill me with the Spirit of God, in wisdom, in understanding, in knowledge and in all manner of workmanship, for creative excellence, in the name of Jesus (Exodus 35:35; Psalm 139:13)

6. We have been created for good works, so I therefore receive divine empowerment to play my part effectively, in the name of Jesus (Ephesians 2:10; Romans 12:6)

7. O Lord, You are the God of all flesh, anoint me to be the best I can be for You, in the name of Jesus (Amos 4:13; Jeremiah 10:12)

8. God that answers prayer, convert my hidden potential to targeted creativity to distinguish me in every season you have placed me, in the name of Jesus (Ephesians 3:20; Psalm 139:14)

9. I refuse to bury my God given talents, but rather choose to use them creatively to serve God and man, in the name of Jesus (Matthew 25:14-29; Daniel 1:17)

10. I receive the mind of Christ for excellence in all thoughts and activities, in the name of Jesus (Philippians 2:5; Isaiah 41:20)

Wisdom To Make Good Decisions

<u>Scripture Reading</u>: Job 12:12; Psalm 37:30; Proverbs 1:7; Proverbs 3:7; Proverbs 13:1

<u>Memory verse/Confession</u>: James 1:5-8

> *"If any of you lacks wisdom, let him ask of God, who gives to all liberally and without reproach, and it will be given to him. But let him ask in faith, with no doubting, for he who doubts is like a wave of the sea driven and tossed by the wind. For let not that man suppose that he will receive anything from the Lord; ⁸ he is a double-minded man, unstable in all his ways."*

<u>Explanation</u>:

Our decisions in life are largely responsible for our choices. This underscores the need for wisdom in our decision-making. These prayers have been carefully put together to help us in our quest for wisdom.

THEME: DECISION DETERMINES DESTINY

1. I receive the power of a made up mind to be decisive in my decision making processes, in Jesus name (Joshua 24:14-15; Joshua 1:8)
2. I do not walk by sight, but by faith, so I walk decisively into my destiny as led by the Spirit of God, in the name of Jesus (2 Corinthians 5:7; Romans 8:14)

3. Doubters are losers, so I refuse to doubt or waiver, but walk boldly into my land of blessing, in the name of Jesus (James 1:5-8; Joshua 1:1-7)

4. I move decisively and promptly in the direction of destiny, and will not procrastinate in Jesus name (Proverbs 4:25-27)

5. Decision determines destiny, so I take hold of destiny and run with it, in Jesus name (Proverbs 4:13-18; Philippians 3:12-14)

6. I receive the wisdom of the ancients and the wisdom that is wiser than my teachers', in the name of Jesus (Psalm 119:99-100)

7. I claim the wisdom that is from above, and reject the wisdom that is from beneath, in the name of Jesus (James 3:13-18; 1 Corinthians 2:13-14)

8. Holy Spirit, anoint me with the wisdom and understanding to succeed in life, in Jesus name (Proverbs 4:5-9; Colossians 2:2-3)

9. I reject the spirit of foolishness and carnality, in the name of Jesus (Ecclesiastes 2:26; 1 Corinthians 1:25)

10. Lord Jesus, as I study to show myself approved, grant me the wisdom which no man can resist, in the name of Jesus (2 Timothy 2:15; 2 Timothy 3:14-17)

Adultery

Scripture Reading: Matthew 5:28; Luke 16:18; John 8:4-11; James 4:17; 1 Corinthians 6:13

Memory Verse/Confession: Exodus 20:14

"You shall not commit adultery."

Explanation:

The Bible and most civilized societies frown upon adultery. It is sexual intercourse between a married man or woman and an individual who is not their spouse. Adultery is very destructive as it is responsible for many broken marriages and the rising rate of divorce. The prayers included in this program are meant to help anyone struggling with the spirit of adultery.

THEME: THE BAIT OF DEATH

1. Lord, deliver me from the trap of the sin of adultery, in the name of Jesus (Proverbs 6:32; Ephesians 5:11)
2. Father Lord, expose and disgrace, every strange man or woman assigned to make me fall, in the name of Jesus (Ephesians 5:11-12: Proverbs 5:3-23)
3. I neutralize by fire, every arrow of lust and seduction fired into my life by any agent of the devil, in the name of Jesus (Proverbs 2:16-20)
4. Holy Spirit, anoint me with the gift of discernment to accurately identify and avoid anyone assigned to lure me into the sin of adultery, in the name of Jesus (Hebrews 13:4)

5. Lord Jesus, help me to die completely to the flesh and it's works and to effectively imbibe and cultivate the fruit of the Spirit, in the name of Jesus (Galatians 5:19-24; Proverbs 5:8-11)

6. I reject the temptation to commit adultery which leads to separation and possible divorce, in the name of Jesus (Matthew 19:9; Proverbs 6:24-29)

7. Holy Spirit, help me to flee sexual immorality and adultery, in the name of Jesus (1 Corinthians 6:18-20; Deuteronomy 22:22)

8. I break free from all forms of youthful lust making me do things I'm not supposed to do, in the name of Jesus (1 Corinthians 10:13; 1 Corinthians 10:8; 1 Thessalonians 4:3-5)

9. Father Lord, cure my heart of the sin of lust that causes me to want to commit adultery, in the name of Jesus (Matthew 5:27-28; 1 Corinthians 7:1-40; Revelations 21:8)

10. I reject the temptation to live in adultery and I claim the grace for sexual purity, in the name of Jesus (Ephesians 5:5; Matthew 19:26; Revelations 2:20-22)

Alcoholism

Scripture Reading: Galatians 5:21; Galatians 5:16; Romans 8:1-2, 14; Romans 14:12; Exodus 34:14

Memory Verse/Confession: Ephesians 5:18

> *"And do not be drunk with wine, in which is dissipation; but be filled with the Spirit,"*

Explanation:

Drinking alcoholic beverages can become addictive, especially when consumed in large quantities. The challenge with alcohol is that apart from being potentially harmful to your health, it can also cause you to lose self-control which may expose you to decisions and actions you may later regret. This may be why the Bible tells us to give strong drink to he who is perishing (Proverbs 31:6). These prayers are designed to help us deal with the problem of alcoholism.

THEME: POWER TO LIVE FREE OF ALCOHOL

1. Father Lord, deliver me from any reliance on alcohol, in Jesus name (Proverbs 20:1)
2. I claim healing from every alcohol related medical condition, in the name of Jesus (1 Peter 2:24; Isaiah 53:4-5)
3. I break myself free of any addiction to alcoholic beverages, in Jesus name (Numbers 6:3; Proverbs 23:20-21)

4. The Bible says give strong drink to he who is ready to perish, so I choose life, and reject death, in the name of Jesus (Proverbs 31:6)

5. I reject every human and spiritual influence that causes me to drink alcohol and drink it to excess, in Jesus name (1Corinthians 6:19)

6. Holy Spirit, I submit totally to Your rule and direction for my life to enable me live above alcoholism, in the name of Jesus (James 4:7)

7. I reject the use of alcohol and the woes associated with it, in the name of Jesus (Isaiah 5:11)

8. Father Lord, deliver me from every form of addiction to alcoholic beverages and the tendency to misuse alcohol, in the name of Jesus (John 8:32, 36; 2 Timothy 4:18)

9. I receive the grace and strength to say no to alcohol and refuse to yield to the temptation to drink too much, in the name of Jesus (Romans 6:16; 1 Corinthians 10:13)

10. Lord, grant me wisdom to identify the destructive nature of alcohol and the boldness to call it what it really is, in the name of Jesus (1 Corinthians 6:12; Romans 13:14)

11. Lord Jesus, help me to mark and avoid every association that pressures and encourages me to drink alcohol, in the name of Jesus (Habakkuk 2:15-16)

Determined To Succeed

<u>Scripture Reading</u>: 1Timothy 6:12; Psalm 37:4; Genesis 39:2-6; Psalm 1:1-3; Proverbs 16:3

<u>Memory verse/Confession</u>: 1 Corinthians 9:24-27

> *"Do you not know that those who run in a race all run, but one receives the prize? Run in such a way that you may obtain it. And everyone who competes for the prize is temperate in all things. Now they do it to obtain a perishable crown, but we for an imperishable crown. Therefore I run thus: not with uncertainty. Thus I fight: not as one who beats the air. But I discipline my body and bring it into subjection, lest, when I have preached to others, I myself should become disqualified."*

<u>Explanation</u>:

The issue of success is a very popular one because everyone is created with the desire to succeed. God put this nature in us and we most times experience frustration when things are not going in our favor. These prayers are meant to help motivate us achieve God's best for our lives, while identifying and helping to eliminate the factors that hinder our success.

THEME: I WILL SUCCEED

1. Anything causing spiritual and physical burnouts in my life, be exposed and terminated completely, in the name of Jesus (Songs of Solomon 2:15; Isaiah 40:30-31)

2. I receive fresh determination and commitment, for maximum input in every department of my life, in the name of Jesus (Acts 10:38; John 14:12)

3. As I increase in my knowledge of God, I receive strength to do manifold exploits, in the name of Jesus (Philippians 4:13; Daniel 11:32)

4. I focus on and take hold of my vision with the eyes and hands of faith and receive the divine ability to accomplish my dream, in Jesus name (Isaiah 48:17; Isaiah 41:10-13)

5. Let the zeal of the house of the Lord consume me for supernatural exploits, in the name of Jesus (John 2:13-17; Colossians 3:23-24)

6. Lord, distinguish me in my business, career, ministry and family life, in the name of Jesus (Isaiah 9:6-7; Ephesians 2:10)

7. Holy Spirit, let your anointing, favor, and mercy, differentiate and distinguish me in the market place of life, in the name of Jesus (Isaiah 61:1-7; Psalm 102:13)

8. I receive uncommon wisdom to exercise proper discernment and discretion in the issues of life, in the name of Jesus (Proverbs 4:5-9; Proverbs 4:23)

9. Lord, endow me with the spirit of excellence and ingenuity to make a difference wherever I go, in Jesus name (Daniel 6:1-3; Daniel 5:10-12)

10. I was created to shine, for I and the children which the Lord has given me are for signs and wonders in Zion, so I arise and begin to shine, in the name of Jesus (Isaiah 60:103; Isaiah 8:18)

Faith To Believe God For The Impossible

<u>Scripture Reading</u>: Hebrews 11:1-6; James 1:3; John 11:25-26, 40; Romans 14:1; John 6:35; Romans 10:10

<u>Memory Verse/Confession</u>: I Peter 1:8-9 (NIV)

> *"Though you have not seen him, you love him; and even though you do not see him now, you believe in him and are filled with an inexpressible and glorious joy, for you are receiving the end result of your faith, the salvation of your souls."*

<u>Explanation:</u>

Faith is important to our Christian walk and life in general. It is so important that God's Word lets us know that without faith it is impossible to please God. Faith is simply taking God at His Word and being able to act on God's Word. The Scriptures also reveal faith can only come by hearing God's Word. These prayers and the accompanying Bible verses are designed to help build our faith.

THEME: FAITH TO MOVE MOUNTAINS

1. Father Lord, I receive the physical evidence of the spiritual realities I have possessed in my prayers, in Jesus name (Mark 11:24)
2. Holy Spirit, open my heart to the faith building potential in the Word of God, in the name of Jesus (James 1:6; Proverbs 4:23; Proverbs 23:7A; Colossians 3:16)

3. O Lord, I know that as faith comes by hearing, fear also comes by hearing, so shut my ears to anything that builds fear in my heart, in Jesus name (Romans 10:17; 2 Timothy 1:7)

4. Lord Jesus, endow me with enough faith to possess the substance of the things I have hoped for, in Jesus name (Hebrew 11:11)

5. I receive the gift of supernatural faith to move mountains in all areas of my life and family, in Jesus name (Mathew 17:20)

6. I choose to have and exercise faith and not doubt God, in the name of Jesus (Matthew 21:21; Matthew 14:31)

7. O Lord, destroy everything in me and around me that suffocates my faith, in the name of Jesus (Songs of Solomon 2:15; Matthew 15:28; 1 Peter 5:9)

8. Holy Spirit, grant me wisdom to surround myself with people that encourage and build my faith, in the name of Jesus (Matthew 9:2-7; Proverbs 13:20)

9. I refuse to dwell on my circumstances and let them discourage me; I choose to concentrate and focus on the greatness and omnipotence of my God instead, in the name of Jesus (2 Corinthians 5:7; Matthew 19:26; Luke 1:37)

10. The Scriptures declare 'The just shall live by faith', so I make a determined effort to live by faith, in the name of Jesus (1 John 5:4; Hebrews 10:38)

Unstoppable Favor

Scripture Reading: Esther 2:8-9, 15-18; Psalm 106:4-5; Psalm 5:12

Memory Verse/Confession: Psalm 102:13

> *"For You, O Lord, will bless the righteous; with favor You will surround him as with a shield."*

Explanation:

Favor points to affirmation or an attitude that expresses itself in approval, goodwill or kindness. Every one desires and needs favor at one time or the other. The prayers contained in this prayer topic have been carefully selected to assist us appropriate the favor of God and man.

THEME: FAVOR THAT CANNOT BE RESISTED OR DENIED

1. Let the favor of God pursue, overtake and bless me in every department of my life, in the name of Jesus (Ephesians 1:11-12)
2. O Lord, arise and favor my Zion, for the time to favor me, yes, the set time has come, in Jesus name (Job 10:12; Psalm 102:13)
3. Father Lord, bless and envelope me with favor like a shield, in the name of Jesus (Psalm 5:12)
4. Let every anti-favor magnet in my life be destroyed, in the name of Jesus Christ
5. I break free from any pattern or cycle of disfavor, in Jesus name (Ephesians 2:8-9)

6. Holy Spirit, touch the heart of all my destiny helpers, to favor me unreservedly, in Jesus name (Genesis 39:3-4)

7. Favor that cannot be resisted be released upon my life now, in the name of Jesus (Psalm 23:5-6)

8. I receive unstoppable and undeniable favor, in the name of Jesus (Psalm 30:5)

9. Destiny helpers assigned to favor and promote me, connect with me and favor me without reservation, in the name of Jesus (Psalm 8:4-6)

10. Favor to out-perform my competitors and rise above my peers and colleagues, locate and distinguish me instantly, in Jesus name (Psalm 75:6-7 KJV)

11. Locational favor to be blessed and celebrated wherever I find myself, promote my destiny from henceforth, in the name of Jesus (Joshua 1:1-3)

12. Every blessing that favor provokes, locate and distinguish me in all areas of my life, in the name of Jesus (Numbers 6:25-26)

13. Men and women of favor from within and outside this nation, connect with me and begin to favor me, in Jesus name (Isaiah 46:11)

14. I receive relationship and marital favor to excel in my relationship and marriage, in the name of Jesus (Proverbs 18:22; Psalm 19:14)

The Fear of The Lord

Scripture Reading: Matthew 10:28; Proverbs 8:13; Ecclesiastes 12:13; Proverbs 14:26; Job 28:28

Memory Verse/Confession: Proverbs 1:7

> *"The fear of the Lord is the beginning of knowledge, but fools despise wisdom and instruction."*

Explanation:

God's Word commands that we have reverential fear for Him. And our love for God and obedience to His laws and dictates should flow naturally from the fact that we fear Him (John 14:15). Below are prayers to inspire us to greater heights in our love, adoration and fear for Him.

THEME: LEARNING THE FEAR OF GOD

1. O Lord, as I fear You, anoint me with the spirit of wisdom, in the name of Jesus (Proverbs 9:10; Psalm 111:10; Psalm 25:14)
2. Holy Spirit, create in me reverential fear for the Lord, in the name of Jesus (Psalm 51:10; Psalm 86:11)
3. I reject ungodly fear, and claim the spirit of power, love, and a sound mind, in Jesus name (2 Timothy 1:7; Isaiah 41:10)
4. Let my fear for God flow from the love I have for Christ, in the name of Jesus (1 John 4:18)
5. I fear the Lord, therefore I choose to obey Him in all things, in the name of Jesus (John 14:15, 21)

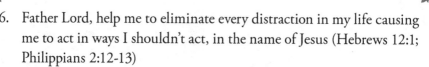

6. Father Lord, help me to eliminate every distraction in my life causing me to act in ways I shouldn't act, in the name of Jesus (Hebrews 12:1; Philippians 2:12-13)

7. Idols in my heart and life that have taken the place of the Lord, I uproot you completely, in the name of Jesus (Ezekiel 14:4-5)

8. Holy Spirit, grant me grace to delight myself fully in You always, in the name of Jesus (Psalm 37:4-7; Psalm 34:9)

9. O Lord, renew Your love in my heart and enable me trust You with all my heart, in the name of Jesus (Proverbs 3:5-8; Proverbs 16:6)

10. Father Lord, as I demonstrate my fear for You by my obedience, bless me beyond my imagination, in the name of Jesus (Psalm 33:8; Deuteronomy 10:12)

11. My Lord and My God, because I fear You I ask that you surround my loved ones and I with Your love and protection, in the name of Jesus (Proverbs 14:27; Luke 1:50)

Power To Get Wealth

<u>Scripture Reading</u>: Proverbs 22:7; Luke 14:28; Luke 6:38; Proverbs 21:20, 13:22; Jeremiah 17:10

<u>Memory Verse/Confession</u>: Luke 6:38

> *"Give, and it will be given to you: good measure, pressed down, shaken together, and running over will be put into your bosom. For with the same measure that you use, it will be measured back to you."*

<u>Explanation</u>:

The issue of wealth creation or the ability to prosper is something that is at the core of our existence, since everyone is not only born with desire to do well, but all of us also have the potential to achieve whatever we aspire to accomplish. These are life-changing prayers anointed to push us into our place of destiny.

THEME: LEARNING TO TAKE CHARGE OF YOUR FINANCES

1. As I tithe and give my freewill offerings faithfully, let the blessings of the covenant overtake and embarrass me, in the name of Jesus (Deuteronomy 28:1-2; Nehemiah 2:20)
2. I break the backbone of the devourer, emptier, and wasters attacking my finances, and decree they will not destroy my ground, in the name of Jesus (Malachi 3:10-12)

3. Holy Spirit, inspire me with new ideas for fresh innovations in my career, finances, business, and ministry, in the name of Jesus (Isaiah 48:17; Joshua 1:8-9)

4. I seal all spiritual holes in my wallet(s), purse(s), pocket(s), and hand(s), with the blood of Jesus, in the name of Jesus (Haggai 1:3-7; Revelation 12:11)

5. O Lord, release unusual favor upon me for financial breakthrough and business success, in the name of Jesus (Psalm 102:13; 106:4-5)

6. Father Lord, grant me the wisdom and power to get wealth, in the name of Jesus (Deuteronomy 8:18; 2 Corinthians 8:9)

7. Father Lord, I know You want me to prosper and be in health, even as my soul prospers, in the name of Jesus (3 John 1:2; Jeremiah 29:11)

8. I decree my God shall supply all my needs according to His riches in glory by Christ Jesus, in the name of Jesus (Philippians 4:19; Psalm 1:1-3)

9. O Lord, I place my total dependence on You and refuse to put my trust in the arm of flesh, in the name of Jesus (2 Corinthians 9:8; Jeremiah 17:5)

10. Father Lord, except You build my life, I build in vain and except You watch over my city, I watch in vain, in the name of Jesus (Psalm 127:1; Job 22:23-27)

Unbroken Focus

<u>Scripture Reading</u>: Matthew 24:13; Luke 10:41-42; 2 Timothy 3:14-17; Colossians 2:6-8; Proverbs 16:3

<u>Memory Verse/Confession</u>: Ecclesiastes 9:10

> *"Whatever your hand finds to do, do it with your might; for there is no work or device or knowledge or wisdom in the grave where you are going."*

<u>Explanation</u>:

Focus points to the ability to stay on task without being distracted from a primary goal or task. As easy as this may sound, remaining focused can be difficult to attain, and it requires a lot training and discipline to achieve. These prayers will help sharpen your focus, while minimizing distractions.

THEME: POWER TO FOCUS AND NOT BE DISTRACTED

1. Let the power of divine focus be released upon me now, in the name of Jesus (Hebrews 12:2)
2. Holy Spirit, identify and get rid of everything that causes distraction in my life, in the name of Jesus (Romans 12:2)
3. I reject the spirit of broken focus attacking my zeal and passion, in the name of Jesus (Hebrews 12:1; Nehemiah 6:1-3)
4. O Lord, help me to keep my eyes on the goal, so I am not diverted, in the name of Jesus (Luke 9:51, 62)

5. I refuse to give myself any alternatives or excuses to quit, that affect my ability to focus, in the name of Jesus (Philippians 3:13-14)

6. I identify and separate myself from everyone confusing and distracting me, in the name of Jesus (Proverbs 13:20; Amos 3:3)

7. Father Lord, grant me wisdom and grace to achieve complete focus in all my endeavors, in the name of Jesus (Proverbs 4:25; 1 Corinthians 15:58, 33)

8. Holy Spirit, help me to always focus on the things that build me up, rather than the things that dissipate my energy, in the name of Jesus (Colossians 3:2; Matthew 6:33; Romans 8:5)

9. I refuse to worry or despair, but choose to trust and focus on the grace of God, in the name of Jesus (Matthew 6:25-32; Philippians 4:13; Philippians 1:6)

10. I choose to focus and be effective, instead of being distracted and becoming unproductive, in the name of Jesus (Matthew 6:24; Proverbs 2:2-5)

Be Fruitful & Multiply

<u>Scripture Reading</u>: John 15:1-27, Galatians 5:21-22, Psalm 92:12-14, Psalm 1:1-6; Matthew 7:7-8

<u>Memory Verse/Confession</u>: Genesis 1:27-28

> *"So God created man in His own image; in the image of God He created him; male and female He created them. Then God blessed them, and God said to them, "Be fruitful and multiply; fill the earth and subdue it; have dominion over the fish of the sea, over the birds of the air, and over every living thing that moves on the earth."*

<u>Explanation</u>:

We were created for fruitfulness and God has pleasure in our prosperity (Psalm 35:27). If we know and strictly follow God's will for our lives, fruitfulness should come naturally. It is when we live and seek to prosper in opposition to His will that we struggle. These are anointed prayers to help us pray our way to fruitfulness.

THEME: PRAYERS TO POSSESS YOUR LAND OF PROMISE

1. I decree that as I serve the Lord my God, He will bless my bread and water, and none shall be barren in my family, in the name of Jesus (Exodus 23:25-26)
2. Let the dew of heaven saturate my land for fruitfulness, in the name of Jesus (Zechariah 8:12; Leviticus 26:9)

3. My Lord & My God, bless me with the fruit of the womb, in the name of Jesus (Deuteronomy 7:12-13)

4. Holy Spirit, breathe upon my life for fruitfulness in all my undertakings, in the name of Jesus (Proverbs 11:30; Deuteronomy 33:13)

5. I prophesy upon my life and family, that we will be fruitful in season and out of season, in the name of Jesus (Isaiah 32:17; Leviticus 26:3-4)

6. Blood of Jesus, address and revoke every curse of barrenness working against my destiny, in the name of Jesus (Deuteronomy 7:14; Revelations 12:11; Hebrews 12:24)

7. I receive the grace to flourish and bear fruit even in old age, in the name of Jesus (Psalm 92:12-15; Genesis 17:6)

8. We receive the blessings of generational fruitfulness in my family line, in the name of Jesus (Ezekiel 19:10; Colossians 1:10)

9. Let the wisdom that comes from God's Word permeate the garden of my life for optimum fruitfulness, in the name of Jesus (James 3:17; John 15:16, 4-5; Matthew 13:23)

10. Father Lord, carefully nurture the tree of my life to produce good fruit, in the name of Jesus (Matthew 7:16-20; John 15:2-3; Genesis 1:11-12)

11. Holy Spirit, whatever needs to die in my flesh for me to be fruitful, let it die, in the name of Jesus (John 12:24; Genesis 22:17)

Learning To Hear God's Voice

<u>Scripture Reading</u>: 1 Samuel 3:19; James 1:19-27; Romans 8:14; 1 Kings 19:11-13; Hebrews 2:1

<u>Memory Verse/Confession</u>: Psalm 32:8-9

> *"I will instruct you and teach you in the way you should go; I will guide you with My eye. Do not be like the horse or like the mule, which have no understanding, which must be harnessed with bit and bridle, else they will not come near you."*

<u>Explanation</u>:

We are created in the image of God to live in intimate relationship with Him. How can you enter or stay in relationship with someone you cannot see, understand or communicate with? So the ability to communicate with God is central to our being able to walk with Him successfully. These prayers will help sharpen our spiritual eyes and ears.

THEME: HEARING GOD CLEARLY

1. I receive the ears of the Prophet Samuel, and the eyes of the Prophet Elisha, in the name of Jesus (1 Samuel 3:10; John 6:63)
2. O Lord, open my spiritual eyes and ears, and the eyes of my understanding in the name of Jesus (Proverbs 2:1-5; Matthew 7:7-8)

3. Holy Spirit, rid my eyes of spiritual cataracts and de-wax my spiritual ears, that I may see and hear You clearly, in the name of Jesus (Exodus 19:9)

4. I decongest and clean out my prophetic pipe by the liquid fire of the Holy Ghost, in the name of Jesus (Hebrews 12:29; Isaiah 30:21)

5. O Lord, help me to discern and hear the voice of God clearly, in the name of Jesus (Mark 4:24; Luke 11:28)

6. Holy Spirit, give me the mind of Christ so I can see, hear and articulate the way Christ did, in the name of Jesus (Philippians 2:5-11; John 8:47)

7. I receive grace and the right connection to hear God clearly, in the name of Jesus (Ephesians 1:17; John 14:16-17)

8. Lord, we have been created with the ability to hear God's voice, so I receive grace to see and hear You clearly, in the name of Jesus (John 10:27; John 16:13)

9. Holy Spirit, enable me to dwell on Your Word richly, so my faith can soar to heights unknown, in the name of Jesus (Colossians 3:16; Romans 10:17)

10. Father Lord, You reveal deep and secret things, grant me the depth of spirit to receive the things you reveal, in the name of Jesus (Daniel 2:22; Psalm 25:14; Jeremiah 33:3)

11. Lord, grant me direction in every area of my life, in the name of Jesus (Isaiah 30:21; Hebrews 4:12)

Be Holy For I Am Holy

<u>Scripture Reading</u>: 1 Peter 2:9; 1 Thessalonians 4:7; 1 John 3:6-10; Psalm 68:4-5; Psalm 103:1

<u>Memory Verse/Confession</u>: 1 Peter 1:14-16

> *"As obedient children, not conforming yourselves to the former lusts, as in your ignorance but as He who called you is holy, you also be holy in all your conduct, 16 because it is written, "Be holy, for I am holy."*

<u>Explanation:</u>

The holiness and love of God are two things that distinguish God from the world and all other beggarly powers. God's holiness presupposes that God cannot sin, lie or be unrighteous. It is the Lord's holiness that portrays Him as a God who is always right and who does not have the capacity to do wrong. This prayer topic will empower us to embrace His holiness.

THEME: THE SPIRIT OF HOLINESS

1. O Lord, help me to follow peace with all men and holiness, without which no man can see You, in the name of Jesus (Hebrews 12:14; Ezekiel 38:23)
2. Let the spirit of holiness and purity, possess and take root in my life, in the name of Jesus (1 Corinthians 6:19; Philippians 2:14-15A)

3. Holy Spirit, create in me the spirit of obedience, that my life may continually be pleasing to God, in the name of Jesus (Romans 12:1; Amos 5:14)

4. God's Word tells me that the wages of sin is death, so I receive the wisdom and power to obey and run from sin, in the name of Jesus (Romans 6:23; Colossians 3:16)

5. Father Lord, I was created in Your image, so I choose to be holy because You are holy, in the name of Jesus (Deuteronomy 26:18-19, 1 Samuel 2:2)

6. Father Lord, help me not to be conformed to this world, but to continually renew my mind by Your Word, in the name of Jesus (Romans 12:2; 2 Corinthians 7:1)

7. O Lord, obedience is the only proof I love You, so help me to obey You completely, in the name of Jesus (John 14:15, 23-24; Ephesians 5:3)

8. Holy Spirit, create in me a clean heart and renew a right spirit within me, in the name of Jesus (Psalm 51:10-12; Psalm 139:23-24)

9. My Lord & My Lord, I choose to live holy just as You are holy, in the name of Jesus (1 Peter 1:15-15; 2 Timothy 1:9)

10. Father Lord, Your Word contains wisdom for life, so I choose to dwell on Your Word, in the name of Jesus (Psalm 119:9; Isaiah 57:15)

The Power of The Holy Ghost

<u>Scripture Reading</u>: John 15:26; Isaiah 28:26; Galatians 5:22-23; Acts 2:38; Isaiah 11:2; Matthew 5:6

<u>Memory Verse/Confession</u>: 1 John 2:27

> *"But the anointing which you have received from Him abides in you, and you do not need that anyone teach you; but as the same anointing teaches you concerning all things, and is true, and is not a lie, and just as it has taught you, you will abide in Him."*

<u>Explanation</u>:

The Holy Ghost is the same Person as the Holy Spirit, the Third Person of the Trinity. When Jesus was about to leave He announced the coming of the Holy Spirit who would indwell, guide and empower us in all things (John 14:16-18). The Holy Spirit is the powerhouse of God. We need the power of the Holy Ghost if we are to be effective in earthly pursuits. These prayers will help you connect with the Holy Spirit like you've never connected with Him.

THEME: THE HOLY SPIRIT ADVANTAGE

1. Holy Spirit, You are the Spirit of truth; guide me into all truth, in the name of Jesus Christ (John 16:12-13; 2 Corinthians 3:17)

2. Spirit of the Most High God, anoint me with power for signs, wonders, and miracles, in the name of Jesus Christ (Acts 10:38; Acts 2:1-5; Acts 1:8)

3. Holy Spirit, open my understanding to God's Word, and open God's Word to my understanding, in the name of Jesus Christ (Luke 24:45-49; Ephesians 1:17)

4. Spirit of God, help and strengthen me in my areas of weakness, in the name of Jesus Christ (Isaiah 40:27-31; Psalm 46:1)

5. Holy Spirit, be my advocate, and comfort me in the battles of life, in the name of Jesus Christ (John 14:16; Luke 11:13)

6. Holy Ghost, teach me all things, and bring to my remembrance all of Christ's Words, in the name of Jesus Christ (John 14:26; 1 Corinthians 2:13)

7. Holy Ghost, revive my spirit with Your fire and love, in the name of Jesus (Isaiah 57:15; Hosea 6:1-3)

8. Power that moves mountains and power to accomplish the impossible, locate and change my situation, in the name of Jesus (Acts 1:8; Matthew 19:26; Luke 1:37)

9. Father Lord, anoint my prayer life and altar with fresh fire for maximum effectiveness and results, in the name of Jesus (Romans 8:26-28; James 5:13-18)

10. Anointing and fire that cannot be insulted, be released upon me now, in the name of Jesus (Deuteronomy 4:24; Psalm 50:15; Isaiah 11:2)

Hope For The Hopeless

<u>Scripture Reading</u>: Romans 12:12; Proverbs 10:28; Proverbs 13:12; Psalm 39:7; Job 17:15

<u>Memory Verse/Confession</u>: Romans 15:13

> *"Now may the God of hope fill you with all joy and peace in believing, that you may abound in hope by the power of the Holy Spirit."*

<u>Explanation</u>:

Hope is the foundation of faith, that is why the Bible says, 'Faith is the substance of things hoped for, the evidence of things not seen' (Hebrews 11:1). God is the God of the hopeless, the One who cares and stands with you when everyone has taken off and left you stranded. If you hold on to Him, you will never be disappointed. These are prayers to encourage and build hope in you.

THEME: HOPE THAT CANNOT BE DISAPPOINTED

1. Father Lord, strengthen my hope in your salvation that my faith may have a solid foundation, in the name of Jesus (Romans 8:24-25; Psalm 71:14)
2. O Lord, because I hope in You to grant my heart's desires, let me receive the substance of things hoped for, in the name of Jesus (Hebrews 11:1A; Romans 5:1-2)
3. Holy Spirit, grant me the grace to keep hope alive, in the name of Jesus

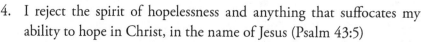

4. I reject the spirit of hopelessness and anything that suffocates my ability to hope in Christ, in the name of Jesus (Psalm 43:5)

5. As I hope in Christ, let me also be able to have faith in Christ to see the evidence of the things I am believing God for, in the name of Jesus (Hebrews 11:1B)

6. Father Lord, grant me the patience and perseverance to wait on You for manifestation, in the name of Jesus (Romans 5:3-5)

7. Lord Jesus, open Your book of remembrance on my account and remember me for good, in the name of Jesus (Esther 6:1-10; Genesis 8:1)

8. My Father, deliver me from a broken spirit and help me to encourage myself in You, in the name of Jesus (Psalm 3:2-5; 1 Samuel 30:1-8; Joshua 10:25)

9. You my soul go back to your resting place and refuse to be troubled, in the name of Jesus (Psalm 11:1-2)

10. Lord, do not allow me to be frustrated in the journey of life, in the name of Jesus (Philippians 4:6-7; Proverbs 10:28)

Humility

<u>Scripture Reading</u>: 1 Corinthians 1:28-29, Matthew 23:12; Matthew 6:2; Psalm 25:8-9; Proverbs 15:33

<u>Memory Verse/Confession</u>: Romans 12:3

> *"For I say, through the grace given to me, to everyone who is among you, not to think of himself more highly than he ought to think, but to think soberly, as God has dealt to each one a measure of faith."*

<u>Explanation</u>:

Humility is a necessary character trait every Christian should have. God abhors pride, but exalts the humble. If your aim is to please God and achieve God's best for your life, you need to train yourself in the art of humility. Humility simply means the ability to debase yourself. I pray these prayers are a blessing to you.

THEME: THE KEY TO DIVINE PROMOTION

1. Let the spirit of lowliness possess my spirit, soul, and body, in the name of Jesus (Psalm 131:1; Proverbs 18:12)
2. I receive the grace to make myself of no reputation, after the order of Jesus Christ, in the name of Jesus (Philippians 2:5-8; Mark 9:35; Micah 6:8)
3. Holy Spirit, break me, mold me, and anoint me with the spirit of humility, in the name of Jesus (Isaiah 57:15; Hosea 6:1-3)

4. I reject and break the yoke of the spirit of pride from my life, in the name of Jesus (Proverbs 16:18; Proverbs 11:2)

5. Lord Jesus, help the flesh in me to decrease, that Your Spirit in me may increase and move unhindered, in the name of Jesus (John 3:30; Galatians 5:16-18)

6. Holy Spirit, grant me a humble and gentle spirit that is patient and accommodative of others, in the name of Jesus (Ephesians 4:1-2; 1 Peter 3:8)

7. Father Lord, help me not to be selfish and over-ambitious, but to display love and selflessness in dealing with others, in the name of Jesus (Philippians 2:3; Romans 12:16)

8. O Lord, grant me the understanding to pursue inward beauty as much as I pursue outward beauty, in the name of Jesus (1 Peter 3:3-4; Galatians 5:22-25)

9. My Lord, as I make a conscious effort to humble myself, promote me according to Your Word, in the name of Jesus (James 4:6-10; 1 Peter 5:5-7; Proverbs 29:23)

10. I put on the helmet of salvation and clothe myself with humility for an effective Christian walk, in the name of Jesus (Ephesians 6:10-18; Colossians 3:12; Proverbs 22:4)

11. Father Lord, grant me wisdom to follow the path of humility and holiness, in the name of Jesus (James 3:13; Matthew 11:28-30; 2 Chronicles 7:14)

The Power of Initiative

Scripture Reading: 1 Corinthians 8:6, Acts 3:15, Acts 2:22, John 5:19; Psalm 119:60; 2 Kings 7:3-8

Memory Verse/Confession: Matthew 7:21

> *"Not everyone who says to Me, 'Lord, Lord,' shall enter the kingdom of heaven, but he who does the will of My Father in heaven."*

Explanation:

Initiative is the ability to operate with minimal or no supervision. It can also be described as the gift of spontaneity by which a person is able to introduce fresh ideas and new ways of getting things done. The Bible says every good and perfect gift comes from our Father above (James 1:17). So we will not be wrong if we say the Holy Spirit is the Spirit of Initiative, since He is the One who teaches us all things and guides us into all truth (John 14:26). These prayers will quicken every dead gift in you and provoke the spirit of initiative for maximum effectiveness.

THEME: THE BLESSINGS OF INITIATIVE

1. Holy Spirit, create in me a sense of purpose and initiative, in the name of Jesus (Proverbs 27:23; Acts 2:39; Romans 4:17; Ecclesiastes 9:10)
2. Let the spirit of initiative for creativity and excellence be released upon me now, in the name of Jesus (Proverbs 6:6-8; 1 Corinthians 2:14)

3. I receive wisdom for initiative that will distinguish me in the market place and God's kingdom, in the name of Jesus (Daniel 6:1-3; James 1:5; Daniel 11:32)

4. O Lord, anoint my mind and thoughts and place me at the top of my game, in the name of Jesus (Acts 10:38; Hebrews 6:11-12; Philippians 4:8)

5. Father Lord, locate and destroy everything that kills initiative in my life, in the name of Jesus (Songs of Solomon 2:15; Matthew 15:13)

6. Father Lord, quicken my spirit, soul and mind to articulate and comprehend as I ought to, in the name of Jesus (Proverbs 23:7A; Proverbs 4:23: 3 John 1:2)

7. I receive the power of initiative to tell right from wrong and to be able to apply knowledge accurately, in the name of Jesus (James 4:17; Proverbs 10:4)

8. I reject everything that causes me to doubt God's gifting and potential in my life, in the name of Jesus (James 1:6-8; 1 Timothy 6:18-19)

9. Let the spirit of boldness to put my initiative to work take hold of my life instantly, in the name of Jesus (James 2:14-18; James 1:23-25; 2 Timothy 1:7)

10. Father Lord, grant me the mindset of service so all I do will be to bless God and humanity, in the name of Jesus (Colossians 3:23-24; 1 John 3:18; 2 Peter 1:5-8; Colossians 3:2)

The Joy of The Lord

<u>Scripture Reading</u>: Romans 12:12; James 1:2-3; Philippians 4:4; Psalm 30:6; Psalm 47:1

<u>Memory Verse/Confession</u>: Psalm 16:11

> *"You will show me the path of life; in Your presence is fullness of joy; at Your right hand are pleasures forevermore."*

<u>Explanation</u>:

Joy reflects a degree of euphoria, elation and happiness. True joy comes from God and our prayer topic is meant to provoke joy in our hearts. May His joy fill your heart as you pray.

THEME: JOY LIKE A RIVER

1. Let righteousness, peace and joy in the Holy Ghost encompass the totality of my being, in the name of Jesus (Romans 14:17; 2 Corinthians 7:4)
2. Joy of the Most High God, be the strength of my life, in the name of Jesus (Nehemiah 8:10B; Isaiah 55:12)
3. My circumstances should not dictate my joy, rather God's love and mercy will dictate my joy, in the name of Jesus (James 1:2; Psalm 118:24)
4. O Lord, expose and disgrace anything assigned to promote sadness in my life, in the name of Jesus (Proverbs 10:28; 1 Thessalonians 2:20)

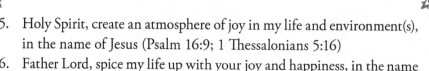
5. Holy Spirit, create an atmosphere of joy in my life and environment(s), in the name of Jesus (Psalm 16:9; 1 Thessalonians 5:16)

6. Father Lord, spice my life up with your joy and happiness, in the name of Jesus (Romans 12:12; Psalm 4:7)

7. Holy Spirit, fill me with all joy and peace as I place my trust totally in You, in the name of Jesus (Romans 15:13; Psalm 33:21)

8. I choose not to be gloomy but to rejoice always, in the name of Jesus (Philippians 4:4; Isaiah 9:3)

9. O Lord, fill my cup of testimony to overflowing as I cry to You daily for intervention, in the name of Jesus (John 16:24; 1 Peter 1:8-9; Ecclesiastes 9:7)

10. Lord, the Bible says a "Joyful heart is full of medicine", so fill my heart with medicine of Your joy, in the name of Jesus (Proverbs 17:22; John 16:22)

11. Father Lord, speedily convert all weeping in my life to joy, in the name of Jesus (Psalm 30:5; 1 John 1:4; 2 John 1:12)

Knowledge Is Power

<u>Scripture Reading</u>: Genesis 2:17; 1 Corinthians 12:8; Colossians 1:9; Proverbs 1:29-33; Proverbs 1:5

<u>Memory Verse/Confession</u>: Proverbs 1:22-23

> *"How long, you simple ones, will you love simplicity? For scorners delight in their scorning, and fools hate knowledge. Turn at my rebuke; surely I will pour out my spirit on you; I will make my words known to you."*

<u>Explanation</u>:

Knowledge is the acquisition of information and skills through education and experience. The acquisition of knowledge positions you for greatness because it sets you above the crowd. This is why it's been said that 'Knowledge is power'. These prayers will help you acquire and filter knowledge.

THEME: BUY THE TRUTH AND DON'T SELL IT

1. Father Lord, grant me in-depth knowledge of Your Word and ways, that I may gain strength to do exploits, in the name of Jesus (Daniel 11:32; Proverbs 2:6)
2. Holy Spirit, guide me into all truth regarding the Person and purpose of Jesus Christ in the name of Jesus (John 14:26; Proverbs 2:1-2)
3. O Lord, as I search, understand, know and practice the truth of Your Word, let the truth set me free, in the name of Jesus (John 8:31-32, 36)

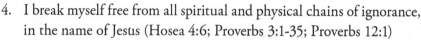

4. I break myself free from all spiritual and physical chains of ignorance, in the name of Jesus (Hosea 4:6; Proverbs 3:1-35; Proverbs 12:1)

5. Lord Jesus, create in me hunger and thirst for knowledge, especially knowledge of God's kingdom, in the name of Jesus (Matthew 5:6)

6. Holy Spirit, instill the fear of the Lord in my heart that I may grow in His wisdom, in the name of Jesus (Proverbs 1:7; Psalm 25:14)

7. Lord, teach me to number my days that I may apply my heart to wisdom, in the name of Jesus (Psalm 90:12; Proverbs 18:15; Psalm 119:66)

8. Wisdom is to seek and apply the knowledge of God's Word accurately, therefore I choose to immerse myself in His Word, in the name of Jesus (Proverbs 15:14; Psalm 19:1-2)

9. I receive the mind of Christ to think and act like Christ, in the name of Jesus (Philippians 2:5; Isaiah 11:2; Proverbs 24:5)

10. The knowledge of wisdom is more precious than riches so I choose to invest in knowledge and wisdom, in the name of Jesus (Proverbs 20:15; Proverbs 2:10; Proverbs 8:10)

Love

Scripture Reading: Songs of Solomon 8:6-7; Philippians 2:2; Psalm 31:16; Psalm 63:3; Psalm 103:13-14

Memory Verse/Confession: Mark 12:30-31

> *"And you shall love the LORD your God with all your heart, with all your soul, with all your mind, and with all your strength.' This is the first commandment. And the second, like it, is this: 'You shall love your neighbor as yourself.' There is no other commandment greater than these."*

Explanation:

Love can be described as affections, emotions and feelings that express themselves in a strong personal attachment. There are different categories of love. The different categories of love are the human relational love, the erotic sensual love and the unconditional God kind of love. These prayers are meant to sensitize our hearts to the ultimate type of love.

THEME: THE POWER OF LOVE

1. O Lord, help me to love You with all my heart, mind, and soul, and to love my neighbor as myself, in the name of Jesus (Psalm 18:1; Romans 13:4-10; Matthew 22:37-39)
2. I receive the grace to love the lovable and unlovable, in the name of Jesus (Luke 6:35; John 14:21-24)

3. Father Lord, enable me to see the lost and unsaved through the lens of the blood of Jesus, that I may love and be willing to pray for and minister to them, in the name of Jesus (Matthew 5:43-48; John 15:9-17)

4. I reject the spirit of hatred, offense and resentment, and claim the spirit of love, in the name of Jesus (Romans 13:8; Galatians 5:13)

5. I choose to forgive all who have wronged me, that God may also be willing to forgive me when I wrong others, in the name of Jesus (Matthew 6:14-15; Colossians 3:14; Proverbs 10:12)

6. Holy Spirit, help me to love and do unto others as I would have them do unto me, in the name of Jesus (Luke 6:31; 1 John 3:1)

7. I receive sincerity of heart to love like Christ loved, in the name of Jesus (Romans 12:9; Philippians 2:5; 1 Corinthians 13:13)

8. Father Lord, grant me the patience and accommodation to bear with my neighbors in love, in the name of Jesus (Ephesians 4:2)

9. I refuse to judge and find fault, but rather choose to love unconditionally, in the name of Jesus (1 Peter 4:7-8; Proverbs 17:17)

10. Let the love of God identify and destroy any form of fear in my heart, in the name of Jesus (1 John 4:18-19; Romans 5:8; Romans 8:37-39)

11. Father Lord, help me to love in deed and not in words alone, in the name of Jesus (1 John 3:16-18; 1 Peter 1:22)

The Wonders of Praise

Scripture Reading: 1 Peter 2:8-9; Hebrews 13:15; Revelations 5:12; Revelations 7:12; Psalm 101:1

Memory Verse/Confession: Psalm 150:1-6

> *"Praise the LORD! Praise God in His sanctuary; praise Him in His mighty firmament! Praise Him for His mighty acts; praise Him according to His excellent greatness! Praise Him with the sound of the trumpet; praise Him with the lute and harp! Praise Him with the timbrel and dance; praise Him with stringed instruments and flutes! Praise Him with loud cymbals; praise Him with clashing cymbals! Let everything that has breath praise the LORD. Praise the LORD!"*

Explanation:

Praise is the expression of heartfelt admiration, elation and outward approval of another. Praise can be for deities, humans, as well as inanimate objects. The praise targeted in this prayer topic is praise for God's greatness and excellence.

THEME: LET EVERYTHING THAT HAS BREATH PRAISE GOD

1. Lord, give me a heart of gratitude that provokes praise for all You have done for me, in the name of Jesus (Exodus 15:2; Deuteronomy 10:21)
2. I thank You Lord for I have breath and life, and so I praise Your name, in the name of Jesus (Judges 5:3; 2 Samuel 22:50)

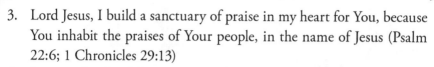

3. Lord Jesus, I build a sanctuary of praise in my heart for You, because You inhabit the praises of Your people, in the name of Jesus (Psalm 22:6; 1 Chronicles 29:13)

4. I praise You Lord, because I am fearfully and wonderfully made, in the name of Jesus (Psalm 139:14)

5. I take every garment of heaviness, and put on the garment of praise, in the name of Jesus (Isaiah 61:3)

6. Father Lord, I will praise and give testimony before the congregation of Your people, in the name of Jesus (Psalm 35:18, 28; Psalm 43:4)

7. Lord, as I enter Your gates with thanksgiving and Your courts with praise, help me to worship You in spirit and in truth, in the name of Jesus (Psalm 100:4; Psalm 92:1; Psalm 138:1)

8. Heal me Lord and I shall be healed, save me as I shall be saved, for You are my praise, in the name of Jesus (Jeremiah 17:14)

9. My Lord and My God, I praise You for Your wisdom and revelation knowledge to me, in the name of Jesus (Daniel 2:22-23; Deuteronomy 23:23; Psalm 25:14

10. God of wisdom and might, I glorify You for Your goodness and mercy towards me, in the name of Jesus (Daniel 4:34; Ephesians 1:3)

The Proper Use of Time

<u>Scripture Reading</u>: Matthew 25:1-46; Matthew 24:36; Proverbs 3:9; Proverbs 3:1-2; Acts 1:7-8

<u>Memory Verse/Confession</u>: Ecclesiastes 3:1

> *"To everything there is a season, a time for every purpose under heaven."*

<u>Explanation</u>:

Time is the most precious resource given to us by God. We all have the same amount of time, but are able to produce different results based on our use and respect for time. These prayers will quicken you and help you to appropriate time more effectively.

THEME: WISDOM TO USE TIME EFFETIVELY

1. O Lord, help me to be at the right place, at the right time, doing the right thing, in the name of Jesus (John 9:4; Psalm 31:14-15)
2. Holy Spirit, give me the right value and sense for time, in the name of Jesus (James 4:13-17; 2 Peter 3:8-14)
3. Father Lord, time is all you've given me to trade with, so help me to use time wisely, in the name of Jesus (Luke 14:28; Psalm 39:4-5)
4. Lord Jesus, help me to number my days, that I may apply my heart to wisdom, in Jesus name (Psalm 90:12; Proverbs 16:9)
5. What I respect works for me, so I choose to respect and use time wisely, in the name of Jesus (Ephesians 5:15-17; Colossians 4:5)

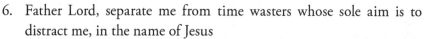

6. Father Lord, separate me from time wasters whose sole aim is to distract me, in the name of Jesus

7. Holy Spirit, grant me the patience to wait on You to guide me, in the name of Jesus (Habakkuk 2:2-3; Romans 8:14)

8. O Lord, You're a God of definite timing; I receive wisdom to understand and flow with God's timing, in the name of Jesus (Isaiah 49:8; John 7:6)

9. Father, there's a time for everything under the sun and I receive grace to walk in perfect harmony with God's time-table for my life, in the name of Jesus (Ecclesiastes 3:1-8; Acts 3:21; Psalm 31:15)

10. Father Lord, hasten to make everything beautiful in my life in a timely manner, in the name of Jesus (Psalm 75:2; Ecclesiastes 3:1)

Genuine Repentance

Scripture Reading: Matthew 4:17; Matthew 21:32; Luke 17:3-4; Luke 24:46-48; Luke 5:31-32

Memory Verse/Confession: Acts 2:38

> *"Then Peter said to them, "Repent, and let every one of you be baptized in the name of Jesus Christ for the remission of sins; and you shall receive the gift of the Holy Spirit."*

Explanation:

Genuine repentance points to a sincere remorse for wrong committed against another. Repentance is turning away from sin or anything that separates us from God. It is because Jesus Christ came to die for our sins that the door of repentance has been opened to us. These prayers are targeted to help us in the area of genuine repentance.

THEME: CREATE IN ME A CLEAN HEART

1. I receive a broken and contrite spirit that is willing to acknowledge wrongdoing and repent when necessary, in the name of Jesus (Psalm 51:17; 2 Chronicles 7:14)
2. Father Lord, forgive and cleanse me of all unrighteousness, as I confess my sins, in the name of Jesus (1 John 1:8-9; Proverbs 28:13)
3. Holy Spirit, always bring to my mind every sin for which I have not repented, and help me to offer thorough repentance, in the name of Jesus (John 14:26; 2 Peter 3:9)

4. O Lord, continually convict me of all wrong doing and keep my conscience sensitive and alive, in the name of Jesus (1 Timothy 4:2; Luke 13:1-5)

5. Lord Jesus, enable me to love and obey You, and make effort to sin less, in the name of Jesus (John 14:15. 23; James 4:8-19)

6. My Lord and My God, enable me to live above self so I do not fulfill the desires of the flesh, in the name of Jesus (Galatians 5:16-18)

7. Father Lord, help me not think more of myself than I ought, but to live in humility towards others, in the name of Jesus (Romans 12:3)

8. O Lord, grant me grace to turn away from my wicked ways, while turning to God in repentance, in the name of Jesus (Acts 3:9; Acts 20:21; Acts 5:31)

9. Thank you Father for providing a concrete pathway to repentance and salvation, in the name of Jesus (Romans 2:4; 2 Corinthians 7:9; Acts 11:18)

10. Lord, let your mercy and conviction not let me stray far before I realize my need for repentance, in the name of Jesus (Jeremiah 31:19; Ezekiel 18:21-23)

Divine Restoration

Scripture Reading: Jeremiah 30:17-22; Psalm 52:12; Acts 3:19-21; Jeremiah 32:27

Memory Verse/Confession: Joel 2:25-26

> *"So I will restore to you the years that the swarming locust has eaten, the crawling locust, the consuming locust, and the chewing locust, my great army which I sent among you. You shall eat in plenty and be satisfied, and praise the name of the LORD your God, who has dealt wondrously with you; and My people shall never be put to shame."*

Explanation:

God's restoration may not come at a time we believe that we desperately need it, but His timing is always perfect. Restoration is re-instatement of things to the way they previously were. These prayers are supposed to enable us to pursue, overtake and recover all we have lost to the enemy.

THEME: RESTORATION

1. Father Lord, restore the years the locust have eaten in my life, in the name of Jesus (Joel 2:25; Psalm 71:20-21)
2. I take back by force all my virtues and glory that have been stolen by the enemy, in the name of Jesus (Isaiah 40:31; Deuteronomy 30:1-10)
3. Let everything Christ died to restore be restored to me instantly, in the name of Jesus (Job 42:10)

4. I provoke divine restoration of all I have lost from when I was in the womb, in the name of Jesus (Psalm 139:13-16; 1 John 5:4; Hosea 6:1-3)

5. Lord, let restoration collide with restoration in my life for a glory explosion, in the name of Jesus (Isaiah 55:10-11)

6. All my benefits currently being detained in witchcraft warehouses, I repossess you by fire, in the name of Jesus (Zechariah 9:12; 1 Peter 5:10)

7. Whatever belongs to me that has been swallowed by serpentine powers, be vomited by fire now, in the name of Jesus (Job 20:15)

8. Marine powers and any satanic body of water holding on to my goodness, let go by force immediately, in the name of Jesus (Psalm 103:1-5; 1 Samuel 30:8)

9. Holy Spirit, restore and breathe life on all dry bones in my life, in the name of Jesus (Ezekiel 37:1-10)

10. The Almighty Restorer of fortunes, restore all my fortunes the wicked one has tampered with, in the name of Jesus (Jeremiah 29:11-14)

The Blessings of Salvation

<u>Scripture Reading</u>: 1 Corinthians 6:9-10; Luke 18:27; 1 Peter 1:8-9; Mark 16:16; Acts 13:47

<u>Memory Verse/Confession</u>: Ephesians 2:8-9

> *"For by grace you have been saved through faith, and that not of yourselves; it is the gift of God, not of works, lest anyone should boast."*

<u>Explanation</u>:

Salvation is God's gift of life to mankind made possible by faith through the grace of God. This grace was expressed through God's love for us that He showed us by the death of His Son on the Cross of Calvary for our sins. So salvation, which is a restoration of our Father-child relationship with God, has been provided. My question is, have you taken advantage of it? These prayers are designed to align us to God's will concerning salvation and Godly living.

THEME: THE FREE GIFT OF SALVATION

1. Lord Jesus, I thank You for saving my soul and counting me worthy of salvation, in Jesus name (Acts 4:12; Titus 2:11-12)
2. Father Lord, help me to continually draw from the well of salvation, in Jesus name (Isaiah 12:3; John 4:5-15)

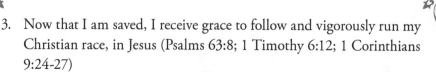

3. Now that I am saved, I receive grace to follow and vigorously run my Christian race, in Jesus (Psalms 63:8; 1 Timothy 6:12; 1 Corinthians 9:24-27)

4. 4. I receive the baptism of the Holy Spirit to be victorious in my Christian walk, in Jesus name (Luke 24:49; Acts 1:8)

5. Lord Jesus, grant me intimacy with You, that I may be led by Your Spirit always, in Jesus name (John 14:15-18; Romans 8:14)

6. Let the joy of salvation fill my heart and soul, and inspire me to be steadfast in things of God, in the name of Jesus (Psalm 51:12; Acts 3:1-10)

7. Father Lord, deliver me from any ungodly lifestyles putting my salvation and ability to make heaven at risk, in the name of Jesus (Ezekiel 18:20-24; Matthew 7:13-14)

8. Holy Spirit, enable me to continually believe that God who saved me by His grace will help me succeed in my Christian walk, in the name of Jesus (Acts 16:30-31; 2 Timothy 1:9)

9. God of my salvation, grant me settlement and rest in You, in the name of Jesus (Psalm 62:1; Romans 5:7-8)

10. Lord Jesus, as I call upon Your name, save and deliver me from my sins, in the name of Jesus (Acts 2:21; 2 Peter 3:9)

Divine Security

Scripture Reading: Psalm 91:1-15; Psalm 121:3-5; 2 Timothy 1:12; Job 19:25-27; Hebrews 6:19

Memory Verse/Confession: Deuteronomy 33:27 (KJV)

> *"The eternal God is thy refuge, and underneath are the everlasting arms: and he shall thrust out the enemy from before thee; and shall say, Destroy them."*

Explanation:

The issue of security is central to human existence since everyone wants to be safe. God is our ultimate source of security, so any attempts to seek security from any other sources are futile exercises. As you pray I am hoping you connect with God's grace on a very personal level.

THEME: DWELLING IN THE SECRET PLACE OF THE MOST HIGH

1. Father Lord, ransom me from the grips of every power holding me captive, in the name of Jesus (Jeremiah 31:10-11)
2. Weapons of the enemy assigned against my security and peace, be roasted by fire, in the name of Jesus (Isaiah 54:17)
3. Father Lord, keep me like the apple of Your eye, in the name of Jesus (Exodus 19:5)

4. Father Lord, protect my destiny, for the bible says except You watch over a city, the watchmen watch in vain, in the name of Jesus (Psalm 127:1-2)

5. Powers attempting to snatch me from the Lord's hands, receive the judgment of fire, in the name of Jesus (John 10:28-29; John 17:12)

6. Whatever has been designed to separate me from the love and protection of the Most High God, receive instant disgrace, in the name of Jesus (Romans 8:35-39)

7. O Lord, You began with me powerfully and You will end with me successfully, in the name of Jesus (Philippians 1:6)

8. Father Lord, Your Word says You're able to save those who come to You, so save me to the uttermost, in the name of Jesus (Hebrews 7:25)

9. Lord, I have put my trust in You, I will not be afraid what man can do to me, in the name of Jesus (Psalm 118:6-7)

10. God, You're my refuge and strength, a very present help in trouble, in the name of Jesus (Psalm 46:1)

The Spirit of Excellence

<u>Scripture Reading</u>: Matthew 28:19; Philippians 4:8; Philippians 1:9-10; Proverbs 27:1-27

<u>Memory Verse/Confession</u>: Daniel 6:3

> *"Then this Daniel distinguished himself above the governors and satraps, because an excellent spirit was in him; and the king gave thought to setting him over the whole realm."*

<u>Explanation</u>:

Excellence is ability to be the best at what you do. It is the process by which we seek to maximize our potential in whatever field we are called to prove ourselves. These prayers will provoke excellence and make us strive to be our best.

THEME: EXHIBITING DILIGENCE IN EVERYTHING

1. Let anointing of excellence rest upon my life in Jesus name (Isaiah 50:4; 2 Peter 1:5)
2. O Lord, help me to be thorough in every assignment I undertake, in Jesus name (Colossians 3:23; 1 Chronicles 4:9A)
3. Holy Spirit, help me to cross my T's and dot my I's in everything I do, in Jesus name (Titus 2:7; 1 John 3:2)
4. I receive the grace to organize myself and be orderly, in the name of Jesus (2 Peter 1:3-4; Proverbs 31:30)

5. I reject disorder and anything that tends to disorganize and unsettle me, in the name of Jesus (Ephesians 2:1-3; Psalm 71:21)

6. I receive an excellent spirit to be at the top of my game, in the name of Jesus (Daniel 5:12)

7. Holy Spirit, grant me grace to excel in everything, especially the things of God, in the name of Jesus (2 Corinthians 8:7)

8. O Lord, every gift you have given me is to serve You and my fellowman, so grant me excellence to serve selflessly, in the name of Jesus (Ephesians 6:7-8)

9. Father Lord, give me understanding of Your Word that I may be the best in everything I do, in the name of Jesus (Joshua 1:8; Colossians 3:16)

10. Lord, as I work on improving my skill, give me access to kings, in the name of Jesus (Proverbs 22:29; Psalm 119:99; Matthew 5:14-16)

The Wonders of Worship

<u>Scripture Reading</u>: 1 Chronicles 11:23-31; Exodus 20:2-6; John 4:21-24; Psalm 99:1-9; Romans 12:1-2

<u>Memory Verse/Confession</u>: Psalm 95:6

> *"Oh come, let us worship and bow down; let us kneel before the LORD our Maker."*

<u>Explanation</u>:

Worship is an act of adoration directed towards another. We are commanded to worship God and God alone. These are prayers of worship and praise to God.

THEME: CREATED TO WORSHIP

1. I take off every garment of heaviness, and put on the garment of worship, in the name of Jesus (Isaiah 60:1-3; Psalm 73:25-26)
2. Father Lord, give me a heart full of gratitude to worship You with reckless abandon, in the name of Jesus (Deuteronomy 29:18; Acts 16:25-26)
3. Holy Spirit, anoint me with the spirit of a worshipper to worship like the twenty-four elders in heaven, in the name of Jesus (Revelations 4:8-11)
4. O Lord, expose and disgrace, everything that attempts to share Your glory in my life, in the name of my Lord Jesus (Nehemiah 9:5-6; Psalm 86:9-10; Daniel 3:16-18)

5. Let the mediations of my heart and the sacrifice of my lips be acceptable in Your sight, in the name of Jesus (Isaiah 29:13; Hebrews 13:15; Psalm 71:8)

6. Lord, I know my obedience is an act of worship, so I choose to obey God, in the name of Jesus (1 Samuel 15:22; John 14:15, 23)

7. Father, I thank You for saving me and giving me Your Holy Spirit, in the name of Jesus (Hebrews 12:28-29; 2 Kings 17:38-39)

8. Lord, I worship You, as I enter Your Gates with thanksgiving and Your courts with praise, in the name of Jesus (Psalm 100:1-5; 1 Chronicles 16:34)

9. Father Lord, You're the Creator of the Universe and My Creator and Redeemer, and I worship You with all my heart, in the name of Jesus (Revelations 14:7; Exodus 23:25-25 NIV)

10. My Lord and My God, I will praise and worship You, for the Bible commands everything that has breath to praise the Lord, in the name of Jesus (Psalm 150:1-6; Isaiah 25:1)

11. I receive inspiration and grace to worship God in spirit and in truth, in the name of Jesus (John 4:24; Psalm 103:1)

12. Lord, as I wait upon You in worship, help me to renew strength, in the name of Jesus (Isaiah 40:31; Psalm 63:1)

Prayers Against Backbiting & Slander

<u>Scripture Reading</u>: Romans 1:28-30; Proverbs 25:23; 2 Corinthians 12:20; 1 Timothy 5:13

<u>Memory Verse/Confession</u>: Psalm 101:5A

> *"Whoever secretly slanders his neighbor, him I will destroy."*

<u>Explanation</u>:

God is love, so if we're created in His image, we were created in the image of love. This is why God is not pleased with backbiting or slander, since it tends to destroy the character and reputation of others created in His image, behind their backs. These prayers are meant to help us overcome and live above these vices.

THEME: OVERCOMING THE SICKNESS OF THE MOUTH

1. O Lord, help me not to say in the absence of anyone what I cannot say in their presence, in Jesus name (James 4:11; Matthew 7:1-7)
2. Father Lord, let me do to others, as I would want them to do to me, in Jesus name (Luke 6:31; Proverbs 16:28)
3. I reject the temptation to slander and backbite, in Jesus name (Psalm 50:20; Leviticus 19:16)
4. Let the fruit of the Spirit possess, control and express itself through my tongue and life, in Jesus name (Galatians 5:19-25; Ephesians 5:4)
5. O Lord, set a guard over my mouth, and keep watch over the door of my lips, in Jesus name (Psalm 141:3; Psalm 34:13; Exodus 20:16)

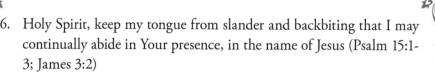

6. Holy Spirit, keep my tongue from slander and backbiting that I may continually abide in Your presence, in the name of Jesus (Psalm 15:1-3; James 3:2)

7. O Lord, I know it is what comes out of my mouth that defiles me so help to only speak words of edification, in the name of Jesus (Mark 7:14-16; Luke 6:45; Isaiah 50:4)

8. I take off and put aside the garment of backbiting and slander, in the name of Jesus (1 Peter 2:1-2; Ephesians 4:29-31; Colossians 3:8)

9. I refuse to be used to cause division amongst others, therefore I will not be part of gossip and slander, in the name of Jesus (Proverbs 26:20; Proverbs 11:9; Galatians 5:15)

10. Holy Spirit, help me not to keep company with slanderers and gossipers, in the name of Jesus (Proverbs 20:19; Revelations 21:8)

Life-Changing Prayers & Supplications

Life is full of challenges, twists, turns and circumstances we're sometimes not prepared to handle. This is why a wise man has said, "Life is fragile, handle it with prayer." The prayers you're about to pray cover a variety of life-related topics. Be sure to prayer with sincerity and focus.

Power To Pursue & Crush My Pursuers

<u>Scripture Reading:</u> Lamentations 5:5; Psalm 35:1-28; Palm 91:1-16; 1 John 4:1; 1 Timothy 4:1

<u>Memory verse/Confession:</u> Ephesians 6:12

> *"For we do not wrestle against flesh and blood, but against principalities, against powers, against the rulers of the darkness of this age, against spiritual hosts of wickedness in the heavenly places."*

<u>Explanation:</u>

Christ came and died to deliver us from the ultimate type of oppression, which is the oppression from the bondage of sin. This freedom empowers us to mount up with wings like eagles and soar above circumstances that attempt to hold us down. We have the power to dominate our lives and environments. These prayers are designed to break the chains of any intrusion into the liberty Jesus has provided us.

THEME: NO CONDEMNATION

1. I sit upon the head of stubborn pursuers permanently, in the name of Jesus (Proverbs 11:8)
2. Arrows of chronic affliction delegated against my peace fail and return to your source, in Jesus name (2 Thessalonians 1:6)
3. Every act of wickedness backed by evil covenants that hinder my progress, I render you powerless, in Jesus name (Isaiah 49:24-26)

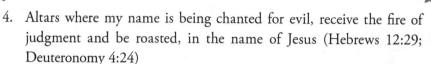

4. Altars where my name is being chanted for evil, receive the fire of judgment and be roasted, in the name of Jesus (Hebrews 12:29; Deuteronomy 4:24)

5. Unrepentant foundational powers pursuing my destiny relentlessly, be disgraced by the blood of Jesus, in Jesus name (Jeremiah 10:11; Revelations 12:11)

6. Every demonic voice opposing my advancement in life, be silenced completely, in the name of Jesus (Lamentations 3:37)

7. Demonic and soulish prayers being offered against my health and peace, backfire now, in the name of Jesus (Isaiah 54:17)

8. I pursue, I overtake and recover all my lost and stolen benefits and blessings, in the name of Jesus (1 Samuel 30:8)

9. Power to locate, enter and possess the land of my blessings, be released upon me, in Jesus name (Joshua 1:1-9)

10. Anointing to manifest the glory heaven has assigned to me, dwell upon me instantly, in Jesus name (Deuteronomy 28:1-14)

11. Every evil conspiracy against me from within and without my circles of influence, scatter by fire, in the name of Jesus (Isaiah 19:1-5; Isaiah 54:15)

Divine Visitation

Scripture Reading: Scripture Reading: 1 Peter 2:12; James 5:14-16; Genesis 18:1-15; Exodus 19:9-11; John 13:17

Memory Verse/Confession: 1 Samuel 2:21

> *"And the LORD visited Hannah, so that she conceived and bore three sons and two daughters. Meanwhile the child Samuel grew before the LORD."*

Explanation:

Divine visitation has to do with God remembering you and turning your captivity around. The Bible says they that call on the name of the Lord shall be saved. So as you call on His name expect great and miraculous things to happen.

THEME: IT'S MY TURN TO REJOICE

1. I step into my season of divine visitation and favored manifestation, in the name of Jesus (James 1:23-25; Deuteronomy 1:6-8)
2. Father Lord, show me a token for good by advertising Your goodness in my life, in the name of Jesus (Psalm 86:17; Psalm 23:6)
3. O Lord, visit me for healing and deliverance and visit my enemies with judgment, in the name of Jesus (Jeremiah 17:14; 2 Samuel 3:1)
4. Wherever I've been rejected I receive grace to be accepted, and wherever I've merely been accepted I receive grace to be celebrated, in Jesus name (Joel 2:25-27; Isaiah 61:7)

5. Covenants and agreements entered into with the sun, the moon and the stars against my increase, I command you to fail by the blood of Jesus, in Jesus name (Isaiah 10:27; Revelations 12:11)

6. Every command given to the earth, the wind, and fire against my destiny, you will not prosper, in Jesus name (Isaiah 7:5-7; Lamentations 3:37)

7. Anyone benefiting from me that has become an Achan in my camp, receive public exposure and disgrace, in Jesus name (Joshua 7:1-26; Revelations 13:10)

8. God of Covenant, begin to load me daily with Your benefits, in the name of Jesus (Psalm 119:60; Colossians 3:23-24)

9. Oh Lord, position my head to receive the maximum amount of Your oil of favor, in the name of Jesus (Psalm 104:13; Psalm 106:4-5)

10. Power to arise and shine in every department of my life, locate me now, in Jesus name (Isaiah 60:1-3; Deuteronomy 8:18)

11. Father Lord, bless and establish me as I believe You and Your prophets, in the name of Jesus (2 Chronicles 20:20; Hosea 10:13)

The God of Elijah

<u>Scripture Reading</u>: 1 Kings 18:20-40; 2 Corinthians 10: 3-6; Romans 13:12-14; Ephesians 6:12

<u>Memory Verse/Confession</u>: Zechariah 4:6

> *"So he answered and said to me:*
> *"This is the word of the LORD to Zerubbabel: '*
> *Not by might nor by power, but by My Spirit,'*
> *Says the LORD of hosts".*

<u>Explanation</u>:

The God of Elijah is an acronym for the God that answers by fire. It symbolizes the power of the Most High God in action. The God of Elijah is a no nonsense God that is ready to do battle on behalf of His children. These prayers are anointed warfare prayers to overcome stubborn situations and enemies.

THEME: THE LORD IS A MAN OF WAR

1. The Lord that answers by fire, answer me by fire today and always, in the name of Jesus (1 Kings 18:24)
2. Fire of Revival, quicken my spirit-man to be the best I can be for You, in the name of Jesus (Leviticus 6:12-13)
3. God of Elijah, renew Your covenant of fire in my life, in the name of Jesus (Hosea 6:1-3)

4. Holy Spirit, revive my prayer and Bible study time by fire, in the name of Jesus (Matthew 7:7 Amplified Bible)

5. Lord Jesus, I receive passion and zeal to be the best I can be for You this year, in Jesus name (Psalm 69:9A)

6. O Lord, create in me a pure heart and renew a right spirit within me, in the name of Jesus (Psalm 51:10)

7. Father Lord, make my feet like the feet of a deer and set me upon my high places, in the name of Jesus (Psalm 18:33; 2 Samuel 22:34)

8. Lord Jesus, let Your zeal and passion possess my heart for maximum commitment, in the name of Jesus (Psalm 69:9; John 2:17)

9. I receive grace to fully understand and obey the will of God, in the name of Jesus (John 14:15, 23)

10. Anointing for signs, wonders and miracles, be released upon me now, in Jesus name (Acts 10:38; Isaiah 8:18)

11. I reject all forms of distraction and claim the wisdom and concentration to focus, in Jesus name (Proverbs 4:27)

The Gates of Hell Shall Not Prevail

Scripture Reading: 1 Peter 2:11; Galatians 5:17; 2 Timothy 3:12; 2 Timothy 6:11-12

Memory Verse/Confession: Luke 22:31-32

> *"And the Lord said, "Simon, Simon! Indeed, Satan has asked for you, that he may sift you as wheat. But I have prayed for you, that your faith should not fail; and when you have returned to Me, strengthen your brethren."*

Explanation:

This is a warfare prayer topic. The gate of hell not prevailing against us is guaranteed with the finished work of our Lord Jesus Christ. It is because of Christ's intercession for us that the gates of hell cannot prevail against us. These prayers will provoke God's power on our behalf.

THEME: VICTORY IS MINE

1. Every friend of darkness in my family, be totally disgraced, in the name of Jesus (Matthew 10:36)
2. Powers following after me to scatter what I have built, my God will scatter you, in Jesus name (Isaiah 54:15)
3. Any bondage originating from the womb, release my destiny by fire, in Jesus name (Psalm 11:3)
4. Attacks from the past making it difficult for me to move forward, I neutralize you completely, in the name of Jesus (Isaiah 10:17)

5. Recurring attacks from my childhood, loose your hold over my life by fire, in the name of Jesus (Nahum 1:13)

6. Collective family yokes promoting unprofitable hard work in my life, break and release me by fire, in the Name of Jesus (Isaiah 47:18; 2 Timothy 4:18)

7. Dream and night related attacks in my life, I arrest you right now, in the Name of Jesus (Matthew 18:18)

8. I melt every pollution in my life by fire and flush them out with the blood of Jesus, in the Name of Jesus (Hebrews 12:29; Revelations 12:11)

9. Powers on assignment to defile me in my sleep, I strangle you with the hands of the Holy Ghost, in Jesus name (Matthew 13:25; Psalm 50:15)

10. I recover everything I have lost as a result of demonic attacks, in Jesus name (1 Samuel 30:8)

11. All my virtues and glory stolen through satanic dreams, I repossess you by fire now, in Jesus name (Job 20:15)

12. Father Lord, unseat every power seating upon the success and growth of my life, in the name of Jesus (Isaiah 59:19)

It's My Time To Celebrate

<u>Scripture Reading</u>: Psalm 145:5; 2 Chronicles 7:1-10; John 15:11; 1 Corinthians 10:31; Ecclesiastes 3:13

<u>Memory Verse/Confession</u>: Psalm 149:5

> *"Let the saints be joyful in glory; let them sing aloud on their beds."*

<u>Explanation</u>:

The Bible clearly tells us that weeping may endure for a night, but joy comes in the morning. What this means is that we have a winning covenant and no matter what happens, we are victorious in Christ Jesus. This is why Romans 8:28 says all things work together for good for those who love God and are called according to His purpose. Your season of celebration has come and these prayers are meant to launch you into that season.

THEME: MY TIME HAS COME

1. Anything standing in the way of my progress, I bulldoze you with the bulldozer of Heaven, in the name of Jesus (Micah 2:12-13; 2 Thessalonians 1:6))
2. Lord, in the presence of those routing for my failure, promote me speedily, in the name of Jesus (Psalm 23:5-6)
3. God of promotion, cause everyone currently looking down on me to begin to look up to me, in the name of Jesus (Psalm 75:6-7)

4. Holy Spirit, You are the Spirit of distinction and originality, distinguish me by signs and wonders in my family, community and nation, in Jesus name (Deuteronomy 26:18-19)

5. God of Relevance, make me relevant in the area of my career, family and calling, in the name of Jesus (Jeremiah 1:10)

6. Spirit of favor, make me outstanding in all I set my hands to do, in the name of Jesus (Acts 7:46-48; Psalm 89:20-37;

7. God of distinction, establish and announce me to my generation by the Spirit of excellence, in the name of Jesus (Daniel 6:3; Daniel 5:1-12)

8. Fountain of Living Waters, flow in me and through me for abundance and breakthrough, in the name of Jesus (Jeremiah 2:13; John 7:38)

9. I walk out of every circle of lack and I walk into my season of plenty, in the name of Jesus (Proverbs 4:18)

10. Power and Grace to accomplish that which has previously been difficult for me, be released on me now, in Jesus name (Acts 10:38; John 14:12)

11. Holy Spirit, bless and promote me to enviable heights, in the name of Jesus (Exodus 23:25-26; Deuteronomy 28:1-14)

From Confession To Possession

Scripture Reading: Proverbs 21:23; Ephesians 4:29; Proverbs 15:1; Proverbs 12:18; James 3:2-10

Memory Verse/Confession: Proverbs 18:20-21

> *"A man's stomach shall be satisfied from the fruit of his mouth; from the produce of his lips he shall be filled. Death and life are in the power of the tongue, and those who love it will eat its fruit."*

Explanation:

God's Word confirms the worlds were created by the power of words. Therefore words have the power to create, and based on the kind of words you're speaking you could be creating a good or bad future. So we need to watch our confession carefully if we are to move in line with God's will and Word.

THEME: THE POWER OF THE TONGUE

1. By the power of the Holy Ghost, I move from confession to possession, in the name of Jesus (Job 22:28-KJV; Psalm 50:15)
2. Lord, convert every positive confession I have ever made to instant testimonies, in Jesus name (Proverbs 12:18)
3. Words spoken against me under demonic authority, I reverse you now, in the name of Jesus (Lamentations 3:37)

4. Negative prophecies spoken against me, locate your sender, in the name of Jesus (Isaiah 54:17)

5. Lord Jesus, let Your Word begin to prosper in every department of my life, in Jesus name (Isaiah 55:10-11)

6. Father Lord, anoint my tongue to provoke the miraculous, in the name of Jesus (James 1:26; 1 Peter 3:10; Job 37:5; Psalm 37:30)

7. Lord pour your oil of greatness upon me, in the name of Jesus (Psalm 71:21; Philippians 4:13)

8. Every secret conspiracy against my advancement, be exposed and disgraced, in Jesus name (Isaiah 54:15)

9. Any invisible hand working for my downfall, wither completely, in Jesus name (1 Kings 13:1-4)

10. Blessings which are due me that are currently delayed, break loose and manifest now, in the name of Jesus (Ezekiel 12:25-28)

11. Holy Spirit, cause me to expand and increase exponentially on all sides, in the name of Jesus (Isaiah 54:2-3)

Possessing My Land of Promise

<u>Scripture Reading</u>: Deuteronomy 30:5; Numbers 33:53; Numbers 34:17; Genesis 22:17; Isaiah 57:13

<u>Memory verse/Confession</u>: Joshua 23:5

> *"And the LORD your God will expel them from before you and drive them out of your sight. So you shall possess their land, as the LORD your God promised you."*

<u>Explanation</u>:

We believers are the Israel of God, just as the Israelites are the Israel of God. And just as the Israelites were chosen by God to inherit a physical land, we have been elected by God to possess a spiritual land. Our success in every other life endeavor is commensurate with our ability to possess this land. These prayers will help us manifest and successfully implement our dominion mandate.

THEME: EXERCISING YOUR DOMINION MANDATE

1. Every land of promise the Lord has prepared for me, I possess you by fire right now, in Jesus name (Leviticus 20:24; Deuteronomy 1:8; Isaiah 54:2-4)
2. I summon my destiny helpers to manifest and help me accomplish God's purpose for my life, in Jesus name (Isaiah 46:11)
3. Every seed of greatness heaven has planted in my life, manifest and make me great, in the name of Jesus (Psalm 8:4-5)

4. I destroy every yoke of 'promise and fail' that is working against me, in the name of Jesus (Numbers 19:23; Proverbs 21:1)

5. Collective family curses working against my life, break and release me by fire, in the name of Jesus (Galatians 3:13; Colossians 2:14)

6. Every rise and fall pattern working against my testimony, perish and release me by fire, in the name of Jesus (Proverbs 4:18)

7. Uncommon favor that will announce me powerfully to my generation, be released upon me now, in Jesus name (Psalm 102:13; Psalm 5:12)

8. O Lord, confuse every mind plotting against me and silence every tongue bad-mouthing me in the place of my breakthrough, in Jesus name (Isaiah 19:1-5; Proverbs 19:21)

9. Holy Spirit, show me a token for good by promoting me beyond my wildest dreams this year, in the name of Jesus (Proverbs 86:17)

10. Let grace for financial favor, increase and expansion, be released upon me immediately, in Jesus name (Deuteronomy 8:18; Isaiah 48:17)

Fresh Oil For New Heights

Scripture Reading: Mark 6:13; James 5:14-16; Hebrews 1:9; Ruth 3:3; Leviticus 4:3; 1 John 2:27

Memory verse/Confession: Psalm 92:10

> *"But my horn You have exalted like a wild ox; I have been anointed with fresh oil."*

Explanation:

Oil is a symbol of God's anointing and power. For reasons of clarity oil is not the Holy Spirit, but a symbol of the anointing and power of the Spirit. These prayers are meant to provoke fresh oil for new heights of glory and achievement.

THEME: POWER TO MOUNT WITH WINGS LIKE AN EAGLE

1. I receive fresh fire for maximum spiritual awakening and vigilance, in the name of Jesus (Isaiah 61:1-3)
2. Any stale oil currently operating in my life, dry up completely, in Jesus name (Matthew 15:13)
3. Holy Spirit, quicken my prayer and Bible reading altar, in Jesus name (Matthew 7:7-8 AMP; 2 Timothy 3:14-16; 2 Timothy 2:15)
4. Father Lord, grant me grace to die to lust and the flesh, in the name of Jesus (Galatians 5:16-18)
5. Lord Jesus, empower me to hate iniquity and love righteousness, in the name of Jesus (Psalm 45:7)

6. Father Lord, help me to identify and get rid of distractions in my Christian walk, in the name of Jesus (Songs of Solomon 2:15)

7. Holy Spirit, open my spiritual eyes and ears and help me to see and hear like You do, in the name of Jesus (1 Samuel 3:1-10; 2 Kings 6:17)

8. O Lord, enable me to value and obey Your word, in the name of Jesus (John 10:27)

9. Lord Jesus, help me not to take Your servants for granted, but cherish and reverence them, in Jesus name (Hebrews 13:17)

10. Holy Spirit, increase my passion and zeal for the things of God, in the name of Jesus (Psalm 69:6-9; John 2:13-17)

11. Father Lord, give me a heart of sacrifice to support the work of God with all my substance, in Jesus name (Proverbs 3:5-11)

12. O Lord, give me a passion for the lost and help me to win souls, in the name of Jesus (Proverbs 11:30)

13. Father Lord, help me to increase my faithfulness and commitment in kingdom matters, in the name of Jesus (Luke 16:10-12)

He Came To Set The Captives Free

<u>Scripture Reading</u>: Isaiah 61:1-3; Isaiah 10:27; Nahum 1:13; Isaiah 59:19; Isaiah 49:24-26; John 10:10

<u>Memory Verse/Confession</u>: Luke 4:18

> *"The Spirit of the LORD is upon Me, because He has anointed Me to preach the Gospel to the poor; He has sent Me to heal the brokenhearted, to proclaim liberty to the captives and recovery of sight to the blind, to set at liberty those who are oppressed."*

<u>Explanation</u>:

Christ came and died to set the captive free. It is because of His life, death, resurrection, ascension and intercession that we are victorious. These are prayers to enable us take advantage of what Christ has done for us.

THEME: FREE INDEED

1. Every chain of captivity holding me bound, break and release me by fire, in the name of Jesus (Nahum 1:13)
2. Stubborn captivity refusing to let go, I demolish you with the hammer of the Word of God, in Jesus Name (Jeremiah 23:29)
3. Any captivity sponsored by wicked covenants, break and release me completely, in Jesus name (Colossians 2:14)
4. I break free from every collective family captivity holding my family in bondage, in the name of Jesus (Isaiah 10:27)

5. Every spirit of slavery that harassed my parents and is harassing me now, release my destiny by fire, in the name of Jesus (Psalm 11:3; Psalm 35:1-28)

6. Generational curses working against breakthroughs in my life, break by the blood of Jesus, in the name of Jesus (Galatians 3:13)

7. Dream related attacks and bondages in my life, be neutralized and release me by fire, in the name of Jesus (Matthew 13:25)

8. Every door of dream defilement the enemy is using to steal from me, I close you completely, in the name of Jesus (Isaiah 49:24-26)

9. Any dream criminal coming to defile me in my sleep, I locate your forehead with the stones of fire, in Jesus name (Isaiah 59:19)

10. Powers of the family idol attacking me from my mother and fathers house, I subdue you by fire and the blood of Jesus, in Jesus name (Jeremiah 10:11)

11. Anyone benefitting from me that is secretly killing me, be exposed and disgraced, in Jesus name (Matthew 10:36; Isaiah 54:15)

12. Every ministry of deceitful friends and relations attacking my destiny, receive fire, in Jesus name (Isaiah 8:9-10-KJV)

13. Any power that wants to send me to an early grave, die in my place, in the name of Jesus (Proverbs 11:8)

14. Father Lord, break every yoke of captivity working against my handiwork and career, in the name of Jesus (Isaiah 48:17)

Favor That Cannot Be Resisted

Scripture Reading: 2 Corinthians 8:9; 2 Corinthians 9:8; Ephesians 1:3; 2 Thessalonians 2:16-17

Memory verse/Confession: Numbers 6:24-26

> *"The LORD bless you and keep you; the LORD make His face shine upon you, and be gracious to you; the LORD lift up His countenance upon you, and give you peace."*

Explanation:

Favor is unmerited. It is God going out His way to bless or help us out when we don't deserve it. This is why favor is so sweet. These prayers will provoke God's favor and that of men in your life.

THEME: FAVORED TO EXCEL

1. Lord, arise and have mercy upon my Zion, for the time to favor me is now, in the name of Jesus (Psalm 102:13; Hebrews 4:16)
2. Bless me Oh Lord, and encompass me with favor as a shield, in the name of Jesus (Psalm 5:12)
3. I tear off every garment of reproach and I put on the garment of uncommon favor, in Jesus name (Isaiah 61:7; Isaiah 60:1-3)
4. As I cry to You O Lord, reduce my labor and increase my favor, in Jesus name (Job 10:12; Titus 3:4-7)

5. Any mark of rejection chasing goodness away from me, be cancelled by the blood of Jesus, in the name of Jesus (Colossians 2:14; Revelations 12:11)

6. Everything in my life and environment attracting hatred and disfavor, I identify and extinguish you by the blood of Jesus, in the name of Jesus (Hebrews 12:24; 1 Peter 2:24)

7. Any stale oil of favor presently operating in my life, dry up completely, in Jesus name (Job 22:28; 2 Peter 1:2-3)

8. Favor that cannot be resisted or stopped, be released upon me now, in the name of Jesus (Psalm 23:5-6; Psalm 103:4-5)

9. Whatever is manipulating God's favor upon my life, release me by fire, in Jesus name (Psalm 30:5; Romans 5:15-17)

10. From today I decree the smell of my life is like the smell of a field which the Lord has blessed, in Jesus name (Genesis 27:27; Jeremiah 33:3; John 17:22-23)

11. I spray my life with the perfume of the Holy Spirit for unusual favor in everything I do, in the name of Jesus (Psalm 8:4-6; Jeremiah 29:11)

12. Holy Spirit, anoint my life with favor that will announce me to this generation, in the name of Jesus (Psalm 75:6-7; 1 Timothy 1:14)

13. Favor of the Most High God, begin to evangelize and attract men and women to me, in Jesus name (Isaiah 46:11; Mark 1:4-5; Acts 2:46-47)

It's My Turn To Be Promoted

<u>Scripture Reading</u>: Psalm 20:4; Colossians 3:23; Psalm 1:1-3; Daniel 2:48; Genesis 12:2; 1 Peter 5:6

<u>Memory verse/Confession</u>: James 4:10

> *"Humble yourselves in the sight of the Lord, and He will lift you up."*

<u>Explanation</u>:

We were created for promotion. God has set us on earth to affect our generation for good. We are the salt and the light of world. We are a city set on a hill and our glory cannot be hidden. What I'm saying is promotion is our heritage and these prayers will position us to take full advantage of this heritage.

THEME: MY SEASON OF EXALTATION

1. Whatever or whoever needs to step down for me to move up, be demoted by fire, in the name of Jesus (Psalm 75:6-7-KJV; Isaiah 54:15)
2. By the blood of Jesus I wipe off every mark of demotion upon my life, in Jesus name (Colossians 2:14; Matthew 15:13)
3. Powers of limitation limiting my progress, go into captivity for my sake, in the name of Jesus (Revelations 13:10; Psalm 75:1-10)
4. Any generational bar set against my progress, be broken by the blood of Jesus, in the name of Jesus (Isaiah 10:27; Revelations 12:11)

5. Familiar spirits monitoring my life for failure, I cage you by fire, in Jesus name (Hebrews 12:29)

6. Satanic embargo programmed against my moving forward, be demolished by the hammer of God's word, in the name of Jesus (Isaiah 59:19)

7. You the month of (insert current month), you are my month of promotion, in the name of Jesus (Job 22:28-KJV; Proverbs 18:20-21)

8. I take back by fire, every good thing that has been stolen from me since I was an infant, in Jesus name (1 Samuel 30:8)

9. Let the spirit of promotion cause everything around me to begin to work for my good, in Jesus name (Psalm 113:7-8; Daniel 3:30)

10. O Lord, cause everyone that is in a position to promote me to begin to cooperate with me, in the name of Jesus (Proverbs 21:1; Isaiah 46:11)

11. Holy Spirit, supernaturally catapult me to my place of promotion, in the name of Jesus (Colossians 1:27; Psalm 78:70-72)

12. Father Lord, silence every voice opposing my promotion, in the name of Jesus (Lamentations 3:37; Proverbs 4:18)

13. Lord, make me an epitome of empowerment and success, in Jesus name (Colossians 1:26; Judges 6:12-16)

14. Holy Spirit, promote my destiny beyond her wildest dreams, in the name of Jesus (Genesis 1:28; Genesis 41:1-45)

Man of War

<u>Scripture Reading</u>: Deuteronomy 20:1-9; Deuteronomy 31:6; Psalm 27:1; Philippians 4:13; James 4:13

<u>Memory verse/Confession</u>: Exodus 15:3

"The LORD is a man of war; the LORD is His name."

<u>Explanation</u>:

The Bible regards the Lord as a man of war. God isn't only a man of war but is the One who fights our battles. God's also tell us He trains our fingers to do battle. These prayers are warfare prayers to help us fight and win the battles of life.

THEME: I AM UNDEFEATABLE

1. MAN OF WAR, go ahead of me in this year and fight my battles for me, in the name of Jesus (Exodus 14:13-14; Deuteronomy 20:1-4)
2. Jehovah Rohi, the Lord of Hosts, become my battle Axe in every battle I am presently facing and crush my enemies, in Jesus name (Isaiah 41:15; Psalm 18:39)
3. Lord, identify every specialized battle assigned against my destiny and neutralize them, in Jesus name (Isaiah 54:17; Deuteronomy 33:27)
4. Angels of Mass Destruction, locate every gathering of my unrepentant enemies for destruction, in the name of Jesus (2 Kings 19:35-36)

5. Any god that did not create the heavens and the earth tormenting my destiny, expire instantly, in the name of Jesus (Jeremiah 10:11; Isaiah 42:13)

6. Any wicked wind programmed against my life, blow back to your sender, in the name of Jesus (Proverbs 11:8; Psalm 34:17)

7. Every crisis initiator causing problems in my life, I dismantle you completely, in the name of Jesus (Isaiah 59:19; Luke 10:19)

8. Programs sponsored against me for frustration, you will not prosper, in the name of Jesus (Isaiah 7:5-7; Isaiah 8:10)

9. Voices chanting incantations against my success, be silenced completely, in Jesus name (Lamentations 3:37; John 10:10)

10. Arrows of infirmity fired by my detractors into my body, jump out by fire and locate your sender, in Jesus name (Revelations 13:10; Psalm 44:5)

11. Every parasite sucking milk and honey from my life, vomit them and expire, in Jesus name (Job 20:15; Isaiah 41:10)

12. Any decree spoken into the atmosphere against my rising, return to your source, in Jesus name (Job 22:28-KJV; Psalm 138:7)

13. Trees of infirmity, planted in any department of my body, be uprooted and wither, in the name of Jesus (Matthew 15:13; 1 John 4:4)

14. Father Lord, release quality men and women into my life for maximum assistance, in Jesus name (Proverbs 21:1; Isaiah 46:11)

Moving Up To Higher Ground

<u>Scripture Reading</u>: Proverbs 5:5-6; Isaiah 43:1-28; Exodus 14:15-16; Psalm 32:8; 2 Corinthians 5:17

<u>Memory Verse/Confession</u>: Philippians 3:12-14

> *"Not that I have already attained, or am already perfected; but I press on, that I may lay hold of that for which Christ Jesus has also laid hold of me. Brethren, I do not count myself to have apprehended; but one thing I do, forgetting those things which are behind and reaching forward to those things which are ahead, I press toward the goal for the prize of the upward call of God in Christ Jesus."*

<u>Explanation</u>:

It is time to move up to higher ground. The Bible confirms that 'Faith is Now' (Hebrews 11:1A), so now and not later is the time to move up. These prayers will help us attain God's best for our lives.

THEME: NO STOPPING ME NOW

1. Every tail anointing militating against my moving up, be cut off completely, in the name of Jesus (Deuteronomy 28:13; Deuteronomy 1:6)
2. Powers of my father's house acting under covenant injunction to bring me down, release me and fall for my sake, in Jesus name (Jeremiah 10:11; 1 John 5:14-15)

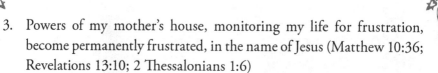

3. Powers of my mother's house, monitoring my life for frustration, become permanently frustrated, in the name of Jesus (Matthew 10:36; Revelations 13:10; 2 Thessalonians 1:6)

4. Foundational covenants that have become a stumbling block to me, break and release me by fire now, in the name of Jesus (Colossians 2:14; Psalm 11:3)

5. Every spirit familiar to my family that is making life difficult for me, go into captivity for my sake, in Jesus name (Matthew 18:18; Hebrews 12:1-2)

6. Holy Spirit, renovate my destiny to align it with your will, in the name of Jesus (Isaiah 61:7)

7. Powers assigned to contend with me at every door of success or accomplishment, receive divine harassment and flee, in the name of Jesus (1 Corinthians 16:9)

8. Anointing of the spiritual eagle and lion be released upon me for success now, in Jesus name (Isaiah 40:31; Revelations 5:5)

9. Lord, begin to reveal to me the deep secrets of my life, in Jesus name (Daniel 2:22; Deuteronomy 29:29)

10. I receive divine empowerment to be who God has created me to be, in the name of Jesus (Daniel 11:32; Isaiah 48:17; Deuteronomy 8:18)

11. Any potential and talent currently hiding in any department of my life, be unveiled for my advantage right now, in the name of Jesus (1 Timothy 4:14; 2 Timothy 1:6)

12. You my life, receive the vision and anointing to achieve what no one else in my bloodline has ever accomplished, in the name of Jesus (Habakkuk 2:2-4; Proverbs 4:25; Isaiah 50:4)

13. Father Lord, renew the revelation and power of Your Word, and increase Your presence in my life, in the name of Jesus (Colossians 3:16; 2 Peter 1:2-3)

Breaking the Backbone of Stubborn Oppression

<u>Scripture Reading</u>: Psalm 9:9; Proverbs 14:31; Zechariah 7:10; Isaiah 1:17; Luke 4:18-19

<u>Memory Verse/Confession</u>: Ecclesiastes 7:7

> *"Surely oppression destroys a wise man's reason, and a bribe debases the heart."*

<u>Explanation</u>:

Oppression can cripple destiny and render a previously glorious destiny unattractive. God is a Deliverer and Savior who delights in setting the captive free (Isaiah 61:1-3). These are prayers to demolish the yoke of oppression.

THEME: I REFUSE TO BE IN CAPTIVITY

1. Every power that has refused to let me go, expire for my sake, in the name of Jesus (Psalm 34:18; Zechariah 9:8)
2. Powers sitting on my ability to prosper, I set your behind on fire, in Jesus name (Psalm 72:4)
3. Covenants and curses from the past, contending with my present and future progress, break and release me by the blood of Jesus, in the name of Jesus (Galatians 3:13; Colossians 2:14)
4. I identify and nullify every word spoken against me under demonic authority, in the name of Jesus name (Isaiah 54:17B; Lamentations 3:37)

5. I break free from every foundational and ancestral stronghold holding me down, in the name of Jesus (Malachi 3:5; Jeremiah 10:11)

6. O Lord, expose and disgrace every ministry of deceitful friends and relationships secretly working against me, in Jesus name (Matthew 10:36; Psalm 45:1-11; Romans 12:19)

7. Anything belonging to me placed on any satanic altar to monitor me, catch fire and burn to ashes, in Jesus name (Deuteronomy 4:24)

8. I wrestle the key of my breakthrough from every evil custodian of the blessings of my family, in Jesus name (Psalm 119:134; Psalm 146:7; Psalm 144:1)

9. Angels of the Living God, cut loose and release to me every blessing allotted to me that is presently hanging, in the name of Jesus (Hebrews 1:14)

10. Fire of God, locate and consume any and every thing sponsoring bewitchment in my life, in Jesus name (Hebrews 12:29; Numbers 23:23; Isaiah 54:14-15)

11. I release my career and destiny from every yoke of limitation, in the name of Jesus (Isaiah 10:27; Nahum 1:13; Psalm 30:4-5)

12. I cover myself with the blood of Jesus, and destroy any power that might want to attack me as a result of these prayers, in Jesus name (Revelations 12:11; Hebrews 12:24)

My Time of Miraculous Advancement

Scripture Reading: Exodus 14:15-16; Psalm 32:8; John 5:8; John 14:6; Isaiah 55:8-9; Job 22:28

Memory Verse/Confession: Isaiah 43:18-19

> *"Do not remember the former things, nor consider the things of old. Behold, I will do a new thing, now it shall spring forth; shall you not know it? I will even make a road in the wilderness and rivers in the desert."*

Explanation:

Advancement is ability to reach God's best for your life. It is achieving success in any endeavor of life. Also, there is worldly and godly advancement. Joshua 1:8 instructs us that by studying, meditating on and practicing God's Word, we will achieve godly success. I see you making giant strides as you pray these prayers aggressively.

THEME: POWER TO MOVE BEYOND OBSTACLES

1. Blessings of the "Dew" of "Heaven" begin to locate and change my life, in Jesus name (Genesis 27:28)
2. You my life, begin to manifest the blessings of a field which the Lord has blessed, in the name of Jesus (Genesis 27:27)
3. O Lord, choose me for unusual blessings and promotion, in the name of Jesus (Psalm 102:13; Psalm 106:4-5)

4. Every divine helper heaven has nominated to help me get to my place of destiny, locate and begin to help me now, in the name of Jesus (Proverbs 21:1; Isaiah 46:11)

5. O Lord, deliver me from dry and desert spirits and seasons, in the name of Jesus (2 Timothy 4:18; Obadiah 1:17)

6. Anything causing me to rise and fall, release my destiny by fire, in the name of Jesus (Nahum 1:13; Isaiah 10:27)

7. Father Lord, repair and restore my direct connection to my heavenly supply, in Jesus name (Joel 2:25-27; 2 Chronicles 7:14)

8. Blood of Jesus, erase completely anything written against me on any demonic blackboard, in Jesus name (Revelations 12:11; Colossians 2:14)

9. Anointing of financial wealth that cannot be resisted or insulted, be released upon me now, in the name of Jesus (Deuteronomy 8:18; Isaiah 48:17)

10. You my destiny, begin to manifest God's will and purpose for you, in Jesus name (Philippians 2:13; Isaiah 8:18)

Supernatural Growth and Expansion For Ministry

<u>Scripture Reading</u>: 2 Timothy 3:14-17; Romans 12:2; 1 Timothy 4:13; 1 Chronicles 16:29

<u>Memory Verse/Confession</u>: 1 Corinthians 3:11

> *"For no other foundation can anyone lay than that which is laid, which is Jesus Christ."*

<u>Explanation</u>:

Christ Himself is the Foundation and Strength of ministry, so we must first learn to minister to Him before we can minister to others. The prayers outlined below are meant to strengthen your hands in ministry.

THEME: THE GATES OF HELL SHALL NOT PREVEAIL

1. Father Lord, strengthen and uphold my ministry with Your right hand of righteousness, in Jesus name (Acts 9:31; Galatians 5:16-26)
2. O Lord, protect and preserve my ministry from every internal and external aggression, in Jesus name (2 Timothy 4:18; Isaiah 5414-15, 17)
3. Father Lord, bring to pass every word You have spoken concerning my life and ministry, in Jesus name (Isaiah 55:10-11)
4. Holy Spirit, convert every prayer and prophecy spoken in my ministry to instant testimonies, in Jesus name (Psalm 20:1-8; Job 22:27-29-KJV)
5. O Lord, release quality men and women into my ministry to help build Your Ministry, in the name of Jesus (Hebrews 3:4; Romans 16:1-27)

6. Holy Spirit, begin to magnetize the sons and daughters of this ministry from the east, west, north, and south and beyond, in Jesus name (John 12:32)

7. Every sheep belonging to this ministry currently in the camp of Laban, de-camp and return back and take your place, in Jesus name (Joel 2:25-27; 1 Samuel 30:8)

8. O Lord, release quality laborers, workers and ministers to help build this ministry, in the name of Jesus (Ephesians 4:11-12; Titus 1:5)

9. Spirit of God, release financial resources and helpers into this ministry to help us build, in the name of Jesus (Matthew 16:18; James 1:17)

10. Father Lord, as you added members daily to the church of the Acts of the Apostles, begin to progressively add members to this ministry, in the name of Jesus (Acts 2:42-47)

Connecting With The Supernatural

<u>Scripture Reading</u>: Isaiah 53:1-12; Numbers 22:5-38; John 17:17; Hebrews 1:14; Job 26:7; Matthew 5:18

<u>Memory Verse/Confession</u>: 1 John 5:14-15

> *"Now this is the confidence that we have in Him, that if we ask anything according to His will, He hears us. And if we know that He hears us, whatever we ask, we know that we have the petitions that we have asked of Him."*

<u>Explanation</u>:

We are creations of the supernatural workings of the power of God, and as such we function best when we have a proper understanding of the supernatural. There are the negative and positive sides of the supernatural, which point to the powers of darkness and light. These prayers are meant to help us provoke the power of the supernatural power of God.

THEME: CREATED FOR SIGNS AND WONDERS

1. Power of the Holy Spirit, do for me what I cannot do for myself this year, in the name of Jesus (Philippians 4:13; Isaiah 65:24)
2. Lord, take me to that mountain higher than my enemies and my flesh, in Jesus name (Psalm 61:2; Psalm 27:5-6)
3. Anointing for signs, wonders and miracles, work for me this year in uncommon proportions, in the name of Jesus (Isaiah 8:18; Mark 16:17-18)

4. God of impossibilities, keep covenant with me this year, in the name of Jesus (Matthew 19:26; Luke 1:37)

5. I receive uncommon ability to succeed where others have failed, and breakthrough where others have broken-down, in Jesus name (Deuteronomy 28:1-14; Psalm 18:29-42)

6. By the workings of God's supernatural power, I enter into my season of celebration, in Jesus name (Isaiah 60:1-3; 10-12; Isaiah 49:23)

7. Every power that will distract me from focusing on God's purpose for my life this year, I arrest you by fire, in the name of Jesus (Proverbs 4:25-27; Songs of Solomon 2:15; Hebrews 12:29)

8. I receive the power of self control and deliverance from the spirit of anger assigned to steal from me, in Jesus name (Ephesians 4:26; 30-32; James 1:19-20; 2 Peter 1:5-9)

9. Spirit of the Most High God, breathe upon all my endeavors for success this year, in the name of Jesus (Genesis 2:7; Psalm 127:1-2)

10. You my life and destiny, receive the supernatural ability to fly on the wings of the Holy Spirit this year, in the name of Jesus (Acts 10:38; John 14:12; Luke 1:37)

Dealing With Obstacles to Success

<u>Scripture Reading</u>: Matthew 16:26-27; Isaiah 41:10; Philippians 4:6-7; Deuteronomy 8:18; Jeremiah 17:7

<u>Memory Verse/Confession</u>: Luke 16:10-11

> *"He who is faithful in what is least is faithful also in much; and he who is unjust in what is least is unjust also in much. Therefore if you have not been faithful in the unrighteous mammon, who will commit to your trust the true riches?"*

<u>Explanation</u>:

Success is part of God's covenant promises for us. The Bible confirms that Christ became poor that through His poverty we might attain the riches of His grace and glory. Paul told the Corinthian church that eye has not seen nor ear heard, nor has it entered into the heart of man what God has prepared for us. As you diligently pray these prayers, it is my hope that God will cause you to connect to success.

THEME: I MOVE FROM OBSCURITY
TO DIVINE PROMINENCE

1. Holy Spirit, identify and neutralize every anti-success deposit in my life, in the name of Jesus (Psalm 18:44-45; Psalm 1:1-3)
2. I disconnect myself from every anti-success syndrome attacking members of my family, in Jesus name (Obadiah 1:17; Psalm 37:4-7)

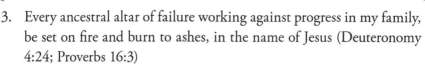

3. Every ancestral altar of failure working against progress in my family, be set on fire and burn to ashes, in the name of Jesus (Deuteronomy 4:24; Proverbs 16:3)

4. I break out of every circle of frustration that has held me captive, in the name of Jesus (Isaiah 10:27; Genesis 39:2-6)

5. Blood of Jesus, locate and erase every mark of rejection sponsoring disgrace in my life, in the name of Jesus (Revelations 12:11; Isaiah 61:7)

6. East wind of God, identify and get rid of anything programmed into the atmosphere to work against my success, in Jesus name (Exodus 14:21-29)

7. Any strongman or woman sitting on my glory, I set your behind on fire, in Jesus name (Hebrews 12:29; Luke 11:21-22)

8. Every power waiting to challenge me at the door of my success, receive the slap of the angels, in Jesus name (1 Corinthians 16:9; 1 Kings 2:3)

9. Arrows of delay fired at the speedy manifestation of my miracle, roast by fire, in the name of Jesus (Ezekiel 12:25-28; Jeremiah 1:11-12-KJV)

10. I attack and demolish the yoke of enchantment bewitching my career, finances, health, education, and relationships, in Jesus name (Exodus 22:18-KJV; Numbers 23:23)

11. You the glory of my destiny, arise and shine instantly, in the name of Jesus (Isaiah 60:1-3; Genesis 1:28-29)

12. I cover myself with the blood of Jesus and destroy any power that might want to attack me as a result of these prayers, in Jesus name (Revelations 12:11; Job 5:12)

It's My Turn To Shine

<u>Scripture Reading</u>: Deuteronomy 30:19; Hebrews 6:1-20; Ephesians 2:8-9; 1 Corinthians 10:13

<u>Memory Verse/Confession</u>: Isaiah 60:1-3

> *"Arise, shine; for your light has come! And the glory of the LORD is risen upon you. For behold, the darkness shall cover the earth, and deep darkness the people; but the LORD will arise over you, and His glory will be seen upon you. The Gentiles shall come to your light, and kings to the brightness of your rising."*

<u>Explanation</u>:

We were redeemed to move from glory to glory. So arising and shining is our heritage and destiny. When we're not living in this promise we really need to check ourselves. These prayers will help you connect to that heritage.

THEME: I WILL ARISE AND SHINE

1. I receive glory and power to mount up with wings like an eagle in every department of my life, in Jesus name (Isaiah 40:31; Ephesians 5:8)
2. Every divine potential buried in me, I command you to arise and begin to shine, in Jesus name (1 Timothy 4:14; Matthew 5:14-16)
3. Any power or person using my virtue to trade, return it now, in the name of Jesus (1 Samuel 30:8; Proverbs 31:1-31)

4. Let every gift God has deposited in me to make me excel, manifest and begin to move my life forward, in the name of Jesus (2 Timothy 1:6; 1 Thessalonians 5:5)

5. Every power holding my key of destiny, release it and expire, in the name of Jesus (Isaiah 49:24-26; Psalm 27:1; Psalm 68:1)

6. I break out of every evil pattern of promise and fail, in the name of Jesus (Genesis 27:40; Acts 1:8)

7. Any PROMISE heaven or anyone has made to me that is yet to be fulfilled, I call forth the fulfillment, in Jesus name (Romans 4:17; Isaiah 55:10-11)

8. O Lord, expose and disgrace every ministry of unfriendly friends working against me, in Jesus name (Daniel 2:22; Deuteronomy 29:29)

9. Father Lord, in the places where men have embarrassed and humiliated me, cause them to celebrate me, in the name of Jesus (Isaiah 61:7; Joel 2:25-27)

10. You my glory, receive divine wings and fly to your place of promise, in Jesus name (John 8:12; Revelations 21:23)

Return To Sender

<u>Scripture Reading</u>: Proverbs 11:8; Proverbs 26:27; Psalm 57:6; Exodus 21:33-34; Psalm 40:2

<u>Memory verse/Confession</u>: Psalm 7:15

> *"He made a pit and dug it out, and has fallen into the ditch which he made."*

<u>Explanation</u>:

God is God of mercy, but is also who repays our enemies in full for their acts of treachery. This prayer program is simply saying that if the enemy won't quit, they should bear the burden of their evil acts. Please pray aggressively.

THEME: THE LAW OF RETRIBUTION

1. Let all the attacks of the wicked directed at me return to the sender, in the name of Jesus (Psalm 35:7-8)
2. Father Lord, cause the enemy to sit upon every unpleasant seat they have prepared for me, in Jesus name (Psalm 9:15)
3. I command every evil plot and conspiracy against me to scatter unto desolation, in the name of Jesus (Isaiah 54:15; Isaiah 8:9-10-KJV)
4. Holy Spirit, expose and disgrace evil conspirators congregating for my sake, in the name of Jesus (Deuteronomy 29:29; Psalm 25:14; Daniel 2:22)

5. Let every power trying to make life unbearable for me receive the heat of the fire of the Holy Ghost, in the name of Jesus (Hebrews 12:29; Psalm 94:12-13)

6. O Lord, destroy every weapon fashioned against me and condemn every tongue rising up in judgment against me, in Jesus name, in the name of Jesus (Isaiah 54:17)

7. I lift up the standard of the Holy Spirit against every flood of the wicked programmed against me, in the name of Jesus (Isaiah 59:19; Job 5:12)

8. My Father and My God, deal with the wicked as they have attempted to deal with me, in the name of Jesus (Jeremiah 18:20-22; Revelations 13:10)

9. Power that raised Jesus Christ from the grave, begin to resurrect all my dead and buried virtues, gifts, and potential, in the name of Jesus (Romans 8:11)

10. Blood of Jesus, erase every mark of affliction inscribed in any part of my body, in Jesus name (Revelations 12:11; Colossians 2:14)

11. Father Lord, contend with every enemy of my soul, in the name of Jesus (Psalm 35:1-10; Isaiah 49:26)

I Mount Up With Wings As An Eagle

<u>Scripture Reading</u>: Job 39:27-30; Hosea 11:1-4; Acts 2:25; Psalm 125:1; Zechariah 8:9; Daniel 7:27

<u>Memory verse/Confession</u>: Isaiah 40:28-31

> *"Have you not known? Have you not heard? The everlasting God, the LORD, the Creator of the ends of the earth, neither faints nor is weary. His understanding is unsearchable. He gives power to the weak, and to those who have no might He increases strength. Even the youths shall faint and be weary, and the young men shall utterly fall, but those who wait on the LORD shall renew their strength; they shall mount up with wings like eagles, they shall run and not be weary, they shall walk and not faint."*

<u>Explanation</u>:

Power to mount up with wings as an eagle comes from the Most High God. This prayer topic is designed to help us access and fully harness the power to mount up with wings as eagles.

THEME: EMPOWERED TO SHINE

1. Supernatural ability of the Holy Spirit to do exploits, be released upon me, in Jesus name (Exodus 19:4; Deuteronomy 32:11)
2. Anointing for signs, wonders and miracles, fall upon me now, in the name of Jesus (Mark 18:17-18; Malachi 4:2)

3. Power for divine possibilities be released upon my life, in Jesus name (Matthew 19:26; Luke 1:37)

4. Holy Spirit, distinguish and set me apart by Your favor, in Jesus name (Psalm 102:13; Psalm 106:4-5)

5. I command the Word of God to become flesh in every area of my life, in the name of Jesus (John 1:1-5, 14)

6. I bring every crisis assigned against my life under the authority of Jesus, the Master of crisis, in Jesus name (1 Peter 5:7; Psalm 55:22)

7. Every knee kneeling against my success, bow to the authority in the name of Jesus, in the name of Jesus (Philippians 2:10-11)

8. O Lord, remove every ungodly label programmed against my life, in Jesus name (Colossians 2:14)

9. Let the glory of the former and latter house be released upon me, in Jesus name (Haggai 2:9)

10. I will arise and shine in every sphere of my life, in the name of Jesus (Isaiah 60:1-3)

11. Mercy of God, make a way for me, in the name of Jesus (Psalm 106:1-2; Psalm 103:1-17)

My Turn To Testify

<u>Scripture Reading</u>: Psalm 71:15-18; Revelations 12:11; Matthew 10:32; 1 John 5:11; Psalm 1:1-3

<u>Memory Verse/Confession</u>: Luke 8:38-39

> *"Now the man from whom the demons had departed begged Him that he might be with Him. But Jesus sent him away, saying, and "Return to your own house, and tell what great things God has done for you" and he went his way and proclaimed throughout the whole city what great things Jesus had done for him."*

<u>Explanation</u>:

We are God's trophies placed on earth to shine forth the light of His glory. Testimony is our heritage and the Spirit of Christ is the engine of our testimonies. These prayers are meant to provoke testimonies in our lives.

THEME: I STEP INTO MY SEASON OF FULFILLMENT

1. Let the heavens agree with the earth to provoke my testimony, in the name of Jesus (Psalm 119:46; Psalm 22:22)
2. O Lord, open the book of remembrance and remember me for good, in Jesus name (Esther 6:1-11)
3. The night has come and gone and I enter into my morning of testimonies, in the name of Jesus (Psalm 30:5; Hebrews 2:12)

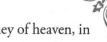

4. Father Lord, sweeten the story of my life with the honey of heaven, in the name of Jesus (Psalm 66:16)

5. O Lord, whatever it will take to change my life and situation, begin to do it now by fire, in Jesus name (Jeremiah 51:10; Psalm 107:10)

6. Holy Spirit, cause my destiny helpers to locate and begin to help me, in the name of Jesus (Isaiah 46:11)

7. I rebuke and arrest every power that causes me to go one step forward and five steps backwards, in the name of Jesus (Proverbs 22:1; Revelations 13:10)

8. Father Lord, disconnect my life from every pattern of disappointment prevalent in my bloodline, in Jesus name (Matthew 10:36; Obadiah 1:17)

9. Any altar before which my name is being chanted for evil, be set on fire instantly, in Jesus name (Jeremiah 10:11; Lamentations 3:37)

10. I receive the key to any goodness God has kept in His bank for me, in the name of Jesus (Revelations 3:7)

11. Holy Spirit, make me a trusted vessel for the display of Your power, in the name of Jesus (Acts 1:8; Psalm 40:9-10)

12. Holy Spirit, anoint my feet to carry me to the land of my breakthroughs, in the name of Jesus (Psalm 92:10; Psalm 71:24; Psalm 35:28)

13. O Lord, make my life a solution to my generation, in the name of Jesus (Matthew 15:14-16)

14. Father Lord, deposit your Spirit and Word of transformation in my life for maximum impact, in the name of Jesus (John 14:26; Colossians 3:16)

I Claim Revival and Fresh Fire

<u>Scripture Reading</u>: Psalm 80:19; Jeremiah 29:12-14; 2 Chronicles 7:14; 2 Timothy 3:1-5; Acts 2:1-47

<u>Memory Verse/Confession</u>: James 4:8-10

> *"Draw near to God and He will draw near to you. Cleanse your hands, you sinners; and purify your hearts, you double-minded. Lament and mourn and weep! Let your laughter be turned to mourning and your joy to gloom. Humble yourselves in the sight of the Lord, and He will lift you up."*

<u>Explanation</u>:

Revival is the process by which the Spirit of God quickens and renews us for continued fellowship with Him, and service to mankind. These prayers have been specially selected to revive our spirit-man.

THEME: POWER TO DO EXPLOITS

1. O Lord, turn me into a prayer machine and convert my prayer life to fire, in the name of Jesus (Luke 11:1-13; Isaiah 41:15; Deuteronomy 4:24)
2. Holy Spirit, create hunger and thirst for God's Word in my heart, in Jesus name (Matthew 5:6; 2 Timothy 2:15; 2 Timothy 3:14-17)
3. Every fire quencher attacking revival in my life, be exposed and disgraced, in Jesus name (Songs of Solomon 2:15; Isaiah 57:15)

4. I receive the passion of Christ to be zealous in all kingdom pursuits, in the name of Jesus (Psalm 69:9; John 2:13-17)

5. O Lord, reconnect me in every area I have disconnected myself from the True Vine, in Jesus name (John 15:1-7; Psalm 85:6; Hosea 6:1-3)

6. I receive the inspiration and grace to serve selflessly, in the name of Jesus (Luke 16:10-11)

7. O Lord, grant me understanding regarding my purpose on earth and help me pursue that purpose vigorously, in the name of Jesus (Romans 8:14; Philippians 2:13)

8. Father Lord, I refuse to be a spectator in the house of God, help me to find my calling and begin to serve immediately, in the name of Jesus (Daniel 2:22; Psalm 25:14; Matthew 7:7-8)

9. Father, encourage and stir up my heart for maximum kingdom investment, in Jesus name (John 10:17-18; Luke 6:38)

10. Lord, As I wait on You, convert my dry bones to flesh, in the name of Jesus (Isaiah 40:27-31; Ezekiel 37:1-14)

Power To Get Wealth

<u>Scripture Reading</u>: Matthew 6:19-21, 24; Proverbs 13:22; Matthew 6:25-33; Ephesians 4:28; Luke 14:28

<u>Memory Verse/Confession</u>: Deuteronomy 28:11

> *"And the LORD will grant you plenty of goods, in the fruit of your body, in the increase of your livestock, and in the produce of your ground, in the land of which the LORD swore to your fathers to give you."*

<u>Explanation</u>:

It is God that gives power and wisdom to get wealth. And the Bible's standard for God's blessings is to seek first the kingdom of God and His righteousness. These prayers have been specially assembled to provoke God's abundant supply. Pray them with all your heart.

THEME: I RECEIVE ACCESS TO MY LAND OF BLESSING

1. I withdraw my destiny from the operation of the spirit of promise and fail, in the name of Jesus (Job 22:28-KJV; Matthew 18:18; Luke 10:19)
2. Wisdom from above for increase and greatness fall upon my life, in Jesus name (Proverbs 4:4-9; James 3:13-17; Proverbs 28:22; 1 Timothy 6:10; Proverbs 21:20)
3. O Lord, distinguish me by your favor in this land, in the name of Jesus (Genesis 26:1-6, 14-16; Psalm 102:13; Psalm 106:4-5)

4. Every ungodly cloud blocking the heavens over my life, be dispersed instantly, in the name of Jesus (Isaiah 10:27; Nahum 1:13; Job 5:12)
5. Holy Spirit, anoint me with creative ideas for breakthrough inventions and products, in Jesus name (Isaiah 50:4; Exodus 31:1-11; Exodus 35:30-35)
6. Every ministry of Judas stealing from my wallet/purse be exposed and disgraced, in Jesus name
7. I break free from every pattern of failure and poverty prevalent in my family, in the name of Jesus (2 Corinthians 8:9; 2 Corinthians 9:8-15)
8. Let the power for finances and wealth acquisition be released upon me, in Jesus name (Luke 6:38; Proverbs 3:9-10)
9. O Lord, on account of my faithful tithing, rebuke the devourer for my sake and prosper my vine, in Jesus name (Malachi 3:8-12; Luke 16:11)
10. I command the grace for unprecedented wealth, increase and expansion to pursue and overtake my life, in Jesus name (Proverbs 22:7; Philippians 4:19; Proverbs 8:18)

Bibliography

The main Scripture for this book is taken from the New King James Version®. Copyright © 1982 by Thomas Nelson. Used by permission. All rights reserved.

This book also contains Scriptures from other different Bible Versions, other than the New King James Version®, which is the principal Scriptural reference

1. "Diseases & Conditions, Liver Disease," Mayo Clinic, http://www.mayoclinic.org/diseases-conditions/liver-problems/basics/symptoms/con-20025300 (15 January 2015)
2. "Signs and Symptoms of Cancer," American Cancer Society, http://www.cancer.org/cancer/cancerbasics/signs-and-symptoms-of-cancer (20 January 2015)
3. "Warning Signs of A Heart Attack," American Heart Association, http://www.webmd.com/hypertension-high-blood-pressure/guide/hypertensive-heart-disease - http://www.heart.org/HEARTORG/Conditions/HeartAttack/WarningSignsofaHeartAttack/Warning-Signs-of-a-Heart-Attack_UCM_002039_Article.jsp (20 January 2015)
4. "Diseases and Conditions: HIV/AIDS," AIDS.gov, https://www.aids.gov/hiv-aids-basics/hiv-aids-101/signs-and-symptoms/ (22 January 2015)
5. "HIV/AIDS Symptoms," Mayo Clinic http://www.mayoclinic.org/diseases-conditions/hiv-aids/basics/symptoms/con-20013732 (22 January 2015)

6. "Symptons of Ebola Virus," Center for Disease Control, http://www.cdc.gov/vhf/ebola/symptoms/ (23 January 2015)

7. "Bone Pain or Tenderness," Medline Plus, http://www.nlm.nih.gov/medlineplus/ency/article/003180.htm (1 February 2015)

8. "Mental Illness and the Family: Recognizing Warning Signs and How to Cope," Mental Health America, http://www.mentalhealthamerica.net/recognizing-warning-signs (22 February 2015)

9. "Diseases and Conditions – Insomnia," Mayo Clinic, http://www.mayoclinic.org/diseases-conditions/insomnia/basics/symptoms/con-20024293 (1 March 2015)

10. "Your Guide to Female Infertility," Web MD, http://www.webmd.com/infertility-and-reproduction/guide/female-infertility (2 March 2015)

11. Shiel, William C, "Infertility Symptom Checker," http://www.medicinenet.com/infertility/symptoms.htm (2 March 2015)

12. "Tumors," The New York Times http://www.nytimes.com/health/guides/disease/tumor/overview.html (15 March 2015)

13. "Signs and Symptoms of Adult Brain and Spinal Cord Tumors," American Cancer Society, http://www.cancer.org/cancer/braincnstumorsinadults/detailedguide/brain-and-spinal-cord-tumors-in-adults-signs-and-symptoms (15 March 2015)

Printed in the USA
CPSIA information can be obtained
at www.ICGtesting.com
LVHW051041131023
760943LV00026B/336/J